Linda Everett

Retro Pies

A Collection of Celebrated
Family Recipes

PORTLAND, OREGON

Design: Jeff Birndorf, endesign
Editor: Aimee Stoddard

Library of Congress Cataloging-in-Publication Data

Everett, Linda, 1946-
   Retro pies : a collection of celebrated family recipes / by Linda Everett.-- 1st American ed.
          p. cm.
Includes index.
   ISBN 1-888054-79-4 (Hardcover : alk. paper)
  1. Pies.   I. Title.
   TX773.E825 2003
   641.8'652--dc21

                                    2003009568

Printed in Singapore

9 8 7 6 5 4 3 2

Collectors Press books are available at special discounts for bulk purchases, premiums, and promotions. Special editions, including personalized inserts or covers, and corporate logos, can be printed in quantity for special purposes. For further information contact: Special Sales, Collectors Press, Inc., P.O. Box 230986, Portland, OR 97281. Toll free: 1-800-423-1848.

For a free catalog write: Collectors Press, Inc., P.O. Box 230986, Portland, OR 97281. Toll free: 1-800-423-1848 or visit our website at: www.collectorspress.com.

Contents

A Little Pie History 7

Pie Crust Clinic 11

Main Dish Pies 15

Fruit Pies 39

Custard Pies 91

Index 126

A Little Pie History

Ever wonder where the old saying "they've cut corners" or "cutting corners" came from? Pie making! Supplies were scarce for the colonists and using a round pan stretched pastry. These early pies were also stretched in another way – the crust itself was thicker and the filling much shallower. The first pies were made from wild fruit and vegetables available in the New World: the predecessor to our Concord grape, blackberries, Salmon berries, pumpkin, native nuts, and a long list of other delights. As orchards began producing a supply of fruit, pies grew in varieties as well as the amount of filling.

Pastry is an ancient invention of the Greeks during their Golden Age. The Romans, tasting a good thing, brought the idea along on their conquests. As the recipe for pastry dough spread throughout Europe, people developed their own adaptations and uses. Over generations the different regions of America found their own specialties – chess and pecan in the South, "quivering" or "nervous" pies (custards) in the Pennsylvania Dutch kitchens, and pumpkin in New England. Pies were an important part of colonial life. Legend has it that once, when a sailing ship was delayed bringing molasses to Connecticut, Thanksgiving was postponed until its arrival so colonial women could bake their traditional pumpkin pies.

Pie history would never be complete without a few words on pie festivities. Pie-supper auctions were once a popular social event. Often held in one-room schoolhouses, young ladies would bake their finest pies and carry them in home-decorated boxes. The auctioneer was a talented ringmaster, teasing and making the crowd laugh. Eager young men would listen for the auctioneer's hints on which eligible girl was the creator of the pie up for bid.

There have always been pie competitions. From colonial days to now, county fairs, church suppers and picnics, bake sales, and other social gatherings have brought out the best in pies. Not too long ago there was a national Cherry Pie contest. Groups like the 4-H and Future Farmers of America continue to keep the judging tables full.

Gramma Griffin's Favorite Pie Dough

My grandmother was one of those cooks who tossed together this and that and served up memorable food. Her biscuits were to die for and her pumpkin pie was the crowning glory of Thanksgiving. Holiday meals were served around her huge oval oak table with a cut glass bowl of camellias in the center.

1 ½ cups all-purpose flour
½ tsp salt
½ cup unsalted butter, chilled
3 to 4 tblsps ice water

In a medium bowl, or in a food processor, mix together flour and salt. Cut butter into small pieces and mix into flour. Add water. Chill dough before rolling out. Makes a single crust for 9 to 10-inch pie.

Yesteryear Pie Dough

This is still the most popular recipe according to old-time cooks. The texture is very flaky. You must be sure the lard is ice cold before using.

1 ⅓ cups all-purpose flour
¼ tsp salt
½ cup lard*
¼ cup ice water
4 tsps cider vinegar

In a medium mixing bowl, combine the flour, salt, and cold lard. Blend as previously described. In a separate cup, mix the ice water and vinegar, then sprinkle over flour mixture and quickly mix in. When dough forms a ball, turn onto a floured board and knead once or twice. Wrap in plastic and chill. Use or refrigerate for 2 days, or freeze for up to 3 months. Makes a single 9-inch crust.

*Lard can usually be found in the dairy department of your store.

Old Faithful Dough

2 ½ cups all-purpose flour
1 tsp salt
1 ½ tsps sugar
1 cup unsalted butter, chilled
4 tblsps shortening, chilled
3 to 4 tablespoons ice water

In a medium bowl, mix flour, sugar, and salt together. Work in butter with pastry knife or your fingers (a food processor works great for this!). Add in shortening and continue cutting in until mixture is crumbly. Sprinkle on ice water and mix with a fork until dough leaves sides of bowl. Turn onto a floured board and knead only two or three times. Overworking makes dough tough. Flatten out dough, cover with plastic wrap and chill for at least 30 minutes. Roll out the dough on a lightly floured surface to the thickness and shape you need. Makes two 8-inch crusts.

Crumb Crust

1 ½ cups crumbs—graham crackers, gingersnaps, vanilla wafers, chocolate wafers, shortbread cookies, or other similar crunchy cookies or wafers—finely crushed

3 tblsps sugar (this varies with the type of cookie you use)

¼ cup + 2 tblsps melted butter

(optional) 1 tsp ground cinnamon, ginger, instant coffee, cocoa powder, nutmeg, pumpkin pie spice, etc.

Preheat oven to 375 degrees.

In a large bowl, combine crumbs, sugar, butter and any spices. Spoon into a 9-inch pie pan and press as evenly as possible to line the pan. Bake for 7 to 10 minutes to set crust. Cool well before filling.

SEE HOW FLAKY
YOUR CRUST CAN BE!

Pie Crust Clinic

if crust is too tough:

1-Too little shortening or too much flour was used.
2-The flour, shortening, and water were not mixed together well enough.
3-The dough was handled or rolled out too much.
4-Too much water was used.
5-The ingredients were measured incorrectly.

if crust is unevenly browned:

1-The crust was not rolled out evenly.
2-Pies were baked too close together.
3-The pie baked too close to oven wall.
4-The filling was not up to top of crust edges.
5-The oven shelf was uneven.
6-The pie baked on too high, or too low, shelf.

if crust fails to brown:

1-The crust was rolled too thin.
2-The dough was overhandled.
3-Too much water was added.
4-Not enough shortening or oil was added.
5-Too much flour was used on the board while rolling out the dough.
6-See list for soggy crust.

if crust is too soggy:

1-The crust was baked at too low a temperature or for too short a time.
2-There was a break or tear in bottom of the crust so filling ran underneath.
3-The filled pie sat too long before it was baked.
4-The pie was placed on a cookie sheet, sheet of aluminum foil, or too shiny of a pie pan, and the heat was deflected from the bottom of pie.

if crust sticks to bottom of pie pan:

1-There was a tear or break in crust that allowed filling to seep through.
2-The filling bubbled over top of the pie and into the bottom of the pan.

if crust doesn't taste right:

1-Too much or not enough salt was used.
2-The crust was overbaked, causing a burnt or scorched flavor.
3-The crust was underbaked, causing a doughy or raw taste.
4-The oil, shortening, or lard were old.

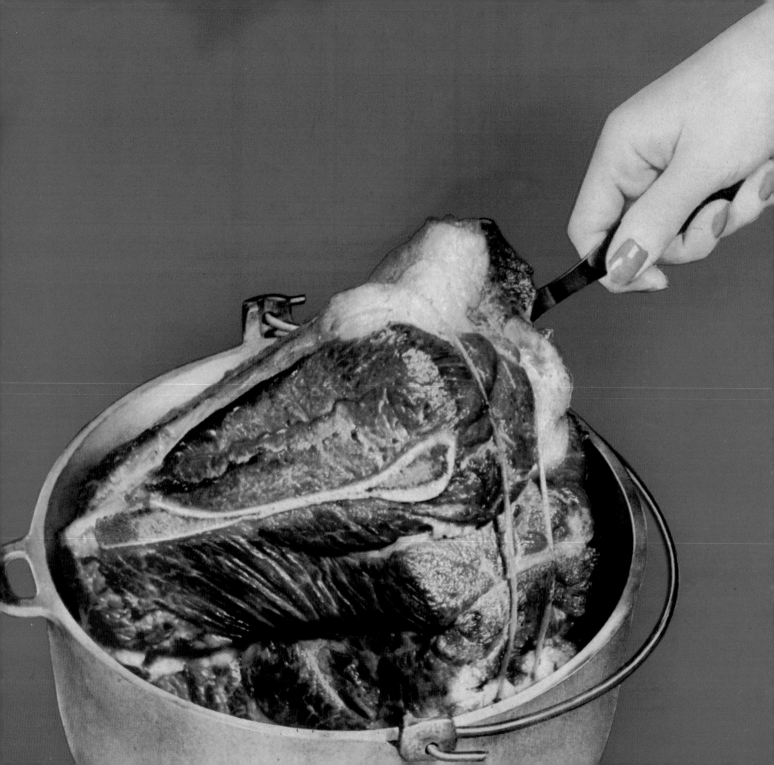

Main Dish Pies

Mystic, Connecticut, is one of those prize locations in America that commands a calendar perfect photo shot from every angle. The picturesque historical shipyards along the Mystic River are home to a fleet of tall, proud sailing ships built by the innovative, intelligent, and hardy men of the sea. This charming town also features numerous buildings (both restored and replicas), demonstrating many aspects of the 18th century seaport life.

Hardy, self-reliant New Englanders brought about equally hearty food utilizing the abundance of the sea. The first recipe (or "receipt," as it was called back then), comes from an 1829 cookbook followed by the modern day version.

Mystic Seaport Clam Pie (Connecticut)

24 fresh clams, Littlenecks, Cherrystone, or whatever is available, shucked

5 tblsps butter

6 tblsps all-purpose flour

2 cups liquid from clams (if there isn't enough add more from bottled clam juice)

⅛ tsp freshly ground black pepper

⅛ tsp ground cloves

Pastry for 8-inch pie with top

Preheat oven to 400 degrees.

In a small saucepan, gently simmer the clams and juice, uncovered, for 5 to 8 minutes. Using a fine-mesh sieve, drain the clams, saving the liquid. Rinse the clams and set aside. In a clean saucepan, melt the butter, remove from heat, and blend in the flour to make a rue. Return to heat and blend until smooth. Take off heat and whisk in the clam liquid, pepper, and cloves. Return to heat and continue whisking until thickened and smooth. Turn down heat to low and let sit for 5 minutes. Stir reserved clams into the sauce, and then pour into pastry shell. Cover with top pastry, making a high fluted edge and holes for steam. Bake 25 to 30 minutes until pastry is golden brown and filling is bubbly. Let stand at room temperature about 5 minutes before serving. Cut into 6 wedges and serve.

New England Portside Pie

4 tblsps butter

15 pearl onions, peeled

½ cup celery, chopped

½ cup all-purpose flour

½ tsp dried thyme

1 ½ cups chicken broth

1 ½ cups milk

½ tsp salt

¼ tsp coarsely ground black pepper

2 boneless, skinless chicken breasts, cooked and cubed

5 to 18 small clams, coarsely chopped

1 package (8 oz.) frozen whole kernel corn, thawed

Pastry for double crust 13 x 9-inch baking dish

Preheat oven to 400 degrees.

In a medium saucepan, melt 1 tablespoon butter and sauté the onions and celery for about 10 minutes. Do not brown. Add in remaining butter with the flour and thyme. Stir for about 1 minute or until thickened. Add in the chicken broth and milk. Cook a few minutes more until mixture forms a nice thick sauce. Stir in salt and pepper. Stir in the chicken, clams, and corn. Pour into the baking dish and top with crust, seal, cut several slits to release steam. Bake for 30 minutes. Crust should be light brown. Serves 6.

Old Sturbridge Clam Pie

Wash the clams well and boil in a gallon of seawater. Shuck. Shake a generous portion of pepper and beaten cloves over them with a lump of butter and a little flour. Make pastry for top and bottom. Fill with clam liquor and cook.

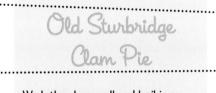

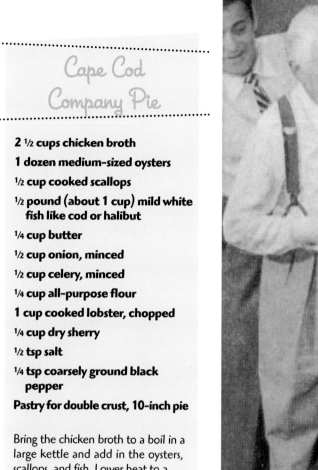

Cape Cod Company Pie

2 ½ cups chicken broth

1 dozen medium-sized oysters

½ cup cooked scallops

½ pound (about 1 cup) mild white fish like cod or halibut

¼ cup butter

½ cup onion, minced

½ cup celery, minced

¼ cup all-purpose flour

1 cup cooked lobster, chopped

¼ cup dry sherry

½ tsp salt

¼ tsp coarsely ground black pepper

Pastry for double crust, 10-inch pie

Bring the chicken broth to a boil in a large kettle and add in the oysters, scallops, and fish. Lower heat to a simmer and cook for another 4 or 5 minutes. Use a slotted spoon and remove seafood to a bowl. Save broth. In a medium saucepan, melt the butter and sauté onion and celery until tender. Stir in flour and continue to stir for about 1 minute. Add in the broth and simmer, stirring, until thick. Gently stir in lobster and sherry. Season with salt and pepper. Set aside. Line a deep dish 10-inch pie pan with half the pastry. Spoon in the seafood filling and top with remaining crust and seal. Cut slits for steam. Bake in oven for about 30 to 35 minutes. Crust should be light brown. Serves 6 to 8.

Oysterville, Washington, is a tiny historic village on the Long Beach Peninsula. Almost every house has a sign stating "Built in 1856" or "Captain So-and-So's house." The house is usually on a picket-fenced lot lined by ancient cedar trees. Surprisingly, Oysterville has a booming oyster business, shipping their product all over the world.

The vast picturesque Willapa Bay serves as the nursery for this tasty treat. The oysters grown nowadays are much larger than the ones the Lewis and Clark expedition dined on. The oysters are now sold at a little walk-up stand with huge mounds of the empty shells nearby and seagulls mooching tidbits. This recipe for an oyster pie is rumored to have its origin in a yesteryear Oysterville kitchen.

Oysterville's Pride

1 pint oysters with their liquid
¼ cup butter
½ cup green pepper, diced (optional)
½ cup celery, diced
1 tsp salt
¼ tsp coarsely ground black pepper
5 tblsp all-purpose flour
2 cups liquid (oyster liquid plus however much milk it takes)
Pastry for single crust 8-inch pie

Preheat oven to 350 degrees.

Drain liquid off oysters and set aside. In a medium skillet, melt butter and sauté green pepper and celery until tender. Stir in salt, pepper, and flour. Cook a few minutes until mixture thickens. Slowly add oyster liquid/milk. Continue cooking until smooth. Add in oysters and spoon into baking or casserole dish. Top with pastry. Bake for 30 minutes until crust is light brown and filling is bubbly. Serves 4 to 6.

Steak and Kidney Pie from Fox N' Hounds Tavern

1 beef kidney, approximately 1 pound
1 pound round steak
2 tblsps butter
1 cup fresh mushrooms, sliced
3 cups water
½ tsp salt
1 bay leaf
1 tsp Worchestershire sauce
3 tblsps all-purpose flour
¼ cup water
Pastry for single 9-inch pie crust

Preheat oven to 375 degrees.

In a medium saucepan, parboil the kidney in salt water for about 15 minutes. Rinse in cold water and dice. Chop the round steak into small pieces. Melt butter in a large skillet or saucepan and brown round steak. Add in mushrooms and cook for an additional 5 minutes. Add water and kidney pieces. Simmer for about an hour with the salt, bay leaf, and Worchestershire sauce. Make a paste of the flour and ¼ cup water and slowly add to meat mixture, stirring constantly. Spoon into baking or casserole dish and cover with crust, seal edges and make a few slits for steam. Bake for 30 to 45 minutes or until crust is light brown. Serves 4 to 6.

Alaskan Tundra Partridge Pie

3 medium size partridges or comparable amount of pheasant, Ptarmigan, pigeon, prairie chicken, grouse, duck or other wild game

½ tsp salt

4 cups water

⅛ tsp coarsely ground black pepper

3 tblsps parsley, minced

¼ tsp dried sage

1 medium onion, chopped

¼ cup salt pork, diced

1 tblsp all-purpose flour

1 tblsp butter

1½ cups potatoes, diced

Pastry for double crust 9-inch pie

Preheat oven to 425 degrees.

Put game birds in saucepan with salt and water. Bring to a boil and skim off any scum. Add in pepper, parsley, sage, onion, and salt pork. Simmer until tender. Add water when needed to keep birds covered. Thicken with flour. Stir in butter. Line a deep baking dish, pie pan, or casserole with pastry. Spoon in half of the potatoes and cover with birds and thickened sauce. Repeat with potatoes and put on top pastry. Cut vents for steam and bake for 35 to 40 minutes or until crust is brown and filling is bubbly. Serves 3 or 4.

Garden Delight Veggie Pie

2 tblsps butter

1 cup onion, chopped

1 cup fresh mushrooms, sliced

1 cup fresh zucchini, sliced

2 tblsps all-purpose flour

½ tsp salt

¼ tsp coarsely ground black pepper

½ tsp dried thyme

2 cups shredded Swiss cheese

1 egg yolk, beaten

3 tblsps water

Preheat oven to 375 degrees.

In a large skillet, melt butter and sauté onion, mushrooms, and zucchini until tender, about 5 minutes. Drain. Stir in flour, salt, pepper, and thyme. Stir until thick. Set aside. Line a 9-inch pie plate with half the pastry. Toss cheese with vegetable mixture and spoon in pie shell. Cover with remaining pastry, seal, and cut slits in top for steam. Beat egg yolk with water and generously brush top of pie. Bake for 45 minutes. Serves 4 to 6.

When the colonists made friends with the Native Americans, they learned the use of many indigenous plants as well as game. The game was plentiful and early cooks made good use of it. The following recipe has been passed down through several generations living in the Winnipesauke Lake area of New Hampshire.

Hunter's Reward

1 cup all-purpose flour
1 tsp salt
¼ tsp ground black pepper
½ tsp ground cinnamon
1 pound venison, diced
½ cup dry red wine or port
1 ½ cups pork sausage
1 cup cooked ham, diced
Pastry for single crust 9-inch pie
1 egg, beaten
¾ cup beef broth, kept hot

Preheat oven to 350 degrees.

In a medium bowl, combine flour, salt, black pepper, and cinnamon. Dredge venison in this mixture and place in a baking dish. Pour over the wine, cover, and bake for 1½ to 2 hours, or until venison is tender. Crumble sausage into the bottom of a deep dish pie pan or similar casserole. Mix ham with the cooked venison mixture and spoon over sausage. Cover pie with pastry, leaving at least one steam vent in center. Baste pastry with the beaten egg. Turn oven to 400 degrees and bake pie for 30 minutes. Pastry should be lightly brown. Pour broth through vent hole in pastry lid and let set for 5 minutes. Serve hot or cold. Serves 4 to 6.

Wintery Favorite Onion Pie

Crust:

1 cup all-purpose flour

¼ pound (1 cube) butter

2 tblsps milk

¼ tsp salt

⅛ tsp pepper

Preheat oven to 350 degrees.

To make crust:
In a medium bowl, combine flour, butter, milk, salt, and pepper. Form into a ball and chill for an hour or two. Roll out for an 8-inch pie pan. Poke generously with a fork and bake for 10 minutes.

Filling:

4 strips lean bacon

2 large sweet onions, chopped (I prefer Walla Walla, Vidalia, or Maui Sweet)

1 egg

1 egg yolk

½ cup sour cream

¼ tsp salt

¼ tsp coarsely ground black pepper

2 tblsps fresh chives, chopped

To make filling:
In a skillet, fry bacon until crisp. Drain well on paper towels and crumble. Cook onions in remaining bacon fat until transparent, but not browned. Drain off fat. In a small bowl, beat together the egg and egg yolk. Mix in sour cream, salt, pepper, and chives. Spoon into baked crust and bake about 20 to 25 minutes, or until filling is firm. Serve warm. Serves 6 to 8.

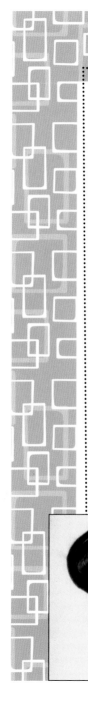

Kansas Sunday Chicken Pie

Filling:
1 large stewing chicken
8 cups water (approximate)
1 medium onion, chopped
1 large carrot, chopped
1 stalk celery, chopped
3 sprigs fresh parsley, about ¼ cup
1 tsp salt
¼ tsp black pepper
2 tblsps butter
2 tblsps chicken fat
5 tblsps all-purpose flour
½ cup cream or half and half

Pastry:
2 cups all-purpose flour
½ tsp salt
4 tsps baking powder
5 tblsps butter
4 tblsps chicken fat
5 tblsps milk

To make filling:
In a large kettle, place chicken, cover with water. Add in onion, carrot, celery, and parsley. Season with salt and pepper. Simmer over low heat about 1½ hours or until chicken is very tender. Let cool. De-bone and discard with skin, saving meat. Strain the broth and skim off fat. Refrigerate fat for later. You will need 3 cups of broth. Pour 1½ cups of broth over chicken meat and set aside. In the top of a double boiler melt butter with 2 tablespoons of chicken fat, stir in flour and stir until thick and smooth, about 2 minutes. Add the remaining 1½ cups broth and stir into double boiler mixture. Continuing stirring until sauce is smooth and thick. Stir in cream and keep warm.

To make pastry:
In a medium bowl, sift together flour, salt, and baking powder. Cut in butter and remaining chicken fat with pastry knife or your fingers. Add milk a little at a time. It should be just enough to hold dough together. Divide pastry in half and roll into a large circle. Preheat oven to 400 degrees. With a slotted spoon remove chicken from its broth and place in bottom of pie. Pour over cream sauce and cover with top pastry. Poke a few steam holes, pinch together edges, and bake for 25 minutes, or until top is golden brown. Serves 4 to 6.

"Chicken-Pye"

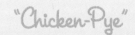

This recipe comes from *The Complete Cook's Guide* cookbook published in Salem, Massachusetts, in 1683. The original version is shown here first, followed by an updated one.

To Make a Chicken-Pye:
After you have truft* your chickens, then break their Legs and Breaft-bones, and raife your cruft of the best Pafte**, lay them in a Coffin***clofe together, with their bodies full of butter, then lay upon and underneath them, Currans, great Raifins, Pruans, Cinnamon, Sugar, whole Mace and Sugar, whole Mace and Salt; then cover all with a good ftore of butter, and fo bake it; then pour into it white wine, rofe-water, fugar, cinnamon, and vinegar mixt together, with Yolks of two or three Eggs beaten amongft it, and fo serve it.

* The letter "f" was used as "s" in colonial times
** Pastry
*** "Coffin" is a baking dish

Colonial Chicken Pie

Chicken:

1 – 3 to 4 pound fryer/roaster chicken, washed

½ cup (1 stick) butter

1 tsp salt

¼ tsp coarsely ground black pepper

¼ cup dried currants

¼ cup raisins

¼ cup dried prunes, chopped

1 tblsp light brown sugar

¾ cup of dry white wine

Sauce:

2 tblsps chicken fat

heart and liver from chicken

½ tsp salt

⅛ tsp pepper

1 tblsp light brown sugar

½ tsp ground cinnamon

¼ tsp ground mace

½ cup dry white wine

1 tblsp apple cider vinegar

1¼ cups cream or half and half

3 egg yolks, lightly beaten

Pastry for single-crust 9 to 10-inch baking dish

Preheat oven to 350 degrees.

To Make Chicken

Remove liver and heart from cavity of bird and refrigerate. Save gizzard and neck for soup on another day. Place ¼ stick butter in cavity and rub chicken with salt and pepper. Place chicken in a baking dish and sprinkle with currants, raisins, prunes, and brown sugar. Pour ¾ cup of the wine over chicken. Dot remaining ¼ stick of butter over the bird. Bake for about 2 hours, basting often with pan drippings. Chicken should be very brown. Test for doneness by wiggling one of the legs and it should detach easily. Remove chicken from pan and cool to temperature you can handle. While chicken cools, make the sauce.

To make the sauce:

In a medium saucepan, melt chicken fat skimmed from pan. Heat until bubbly. Mince chicken heart and liver and sauté for 2 to 3 minutes in pan. Add in the salt, pepper, brown sugar, cinnamon, mace, wine, and the vinegar. Simmer, uncovered, until liquid is reduced by about half. Meanwhile, remove meat from bones and cut in generous bite-size pieces. With a slotted spoon remove currants, raisins, and prunes from pan and set aside. Pour drippings in a measuring cup and add enough cream to make 2½ cups. Blend in egg yolks. Mix a small amount of this mixture with about ¼ cup of the liver/heart sauce and blend all back into the saucepan and heat over low for about 1 minute. Mixture should thicken. Stir in currants, raisins, and prunes. Layer chicken pieces in a 9 to 10-inch (diameter) baking dish. Pour on sauce. Top with pastry, moistening edge of dish and sealing on crust. Cut steam vents and bake for 45 to 50 minutes. Pie should be golden brown with bubbly filling. Serves 6 to 8.

Perhaps you believe the nursery rhyme "Four and twenty black birds baked in a pie" is only a bit of myth. The truth is twenty-four black birds, doves, quail, squab, or other small game birds are exactly right for six guests. Since hunting black birds, as well as many other small birds, is illegal these days, following the original recipe isn't possible. However, game hens are a good substitute. This recipe comes from early settlers in Florida who used red-winged black birds or rice birds for this traditional pie.

Filling:

- 6 – ½ pound (approximately) game hens, or equivalent in doves or other wild game birds
- 6 tblsps butter
- 2 cups hot water
- 1 bay leaf
- 1 tsp salt
- ¼ tsp black pepper
- 1 large carrot, peeled, cut in strips
- 12 small whole onions, peeled
- 6 small whole white potatoes, diced
- 4 tblsps all-purpose flour
- ¼ cup water
- 2 tblsps fresh parsley, minced
- 1 cup sherry

Crust:

- 2 cups all-purpose flour
- 5 tsps baking powder
- 1 tsp salt
- 4 tblsps butter
- 1 cup milk (approximately)

To make the filling:

Wash and pat dry game hens. Cut in half lengthwise. In a large heavy skillet, melt butter and brown birds on all sides. Cover with hot water and add in bay leaf, salt, and pepper. Cover tightly and simmer over low heat until game hens are tender, about 25 minutes. Add in carrot and onions and simmer another 10 minutes. Add in potatoes, parsley, and sherry and simmer another 15 minutes. Add more water if necessary. There should be enough liquid to cover ingredients. Preheat oven to 400 degrees. Mix flour with water and gently stir into chicken mixture. Spoon filling into a deep casserole dish and top with crust (see recipe below), and bake 20 minutes or until crust is browned. Serves 6.

To make the crust:

In a medium bowl, sift together the flour, baking powder, and salt. Cut in butter with a pastry cutter or your fingers. Dough should be crumbly. Add in milk, a little at a time, until dough sticks together. Turn out on floured board and knead twice. Roll to ½ inch thick and cover casserole dish, crimping edges, and sealing well. Cut steam vents.

This recipe dates as far back as 1824. The once prosperous crossroad town of Washington, Arkansas, hosted such celebrated guests as Stephen Austin, Sam Houston, and Jim Bowie. Legend has it the famous Bowie knife was first forged by local blacksmith Jim Black. This simple frugal recipe was intended to use up leftovers.

Old Arkaansas Boiled Egg Pie

1 ½ tblsps butter

⅓ cup celery, minced

¼ cup onion, minced

1 tblsp all-purpose flour

1 ¼ cups light cream or half and half

¾ cup grated sharp cheddar cheese

½ cup cooked peas

1 tsp salt

⅛ tsp black pepper

2 egg yolks, lightly beaten

2 tblsps dry sherry

6 hard-boiled eggs

Pastry for 2-crust 9-inch pie (See pages 8-9)

Preheat oven to 400 degrees.

To make the crust:
Make pastry cutouts in rounds, leaves, or whatever you like, using cookie cutter. Bake these on baking sheet along with the bottom crust, (don't forget to prick the crust and crimp with a high fluted edge), for 8 to 10 minutes. Cool.

To make the filling:
In a medium saucepan, melt the butter and sauté celery and onion until tender. Blend in the flour. Add cream and stir over low heat until thick, about 3 minutes. Stir in the cheese, peas, salt, and pepper. Mix a small amount of egg yolk in mixture, and then stir back in. Stir in sherry. Remove from heat. Slice hard-boiled eggs and arrange around in pie crust. Pour over cheese mixture and place baked pastry cut-outs over top. Return to 375 degree oven and bake 15 to 20 minutes until filling bubbles. Let stand a few minutes before cutting. Makes 6 servings.

Creole Pork Pie

pastry for a 2-crust pie (See pages 8-9)

4 tart green apples, like Pippin or Granny Smith, pared, cored, sliced

2 pounds lean pork, cubed

2 tblsps brown sugar

½ tsp dried thyme

1 tsp salt

¼ tsp coarsely ground black pepper

1 tblsp butter

1 egg, well beaten

Preheat oven to 350 degrees.

Line bottom and sides of deep dish pie pan with pastry. Line dish with apple slices and layer over with pork. In a small bowl, combine brown sugar, thyme, salt, and pepper and sprinkle over all. Continue layering. Dot the top with butter and cover with pastry. Pinch edges and slash top. Brush top generously with beaten egg. Bake for 1½ to 2 hours until bubbly and golden brown. Serves 4 to 6.

This recipe came from the old streets of New Orleans in the 1800s. Some cooks bragged this was a way of feeding "the boys" both their mainstay meat dish and apple pie, too.

Truth is, the first Thanksgiving meal was probably not served with a wild turkey as the crowning glory. The feast probably had fish and other game, as well as maize (corn), squash, and numerous native vegetables and fruits. The story of our ancestors feasting on leftover Thanksgiving turkey more than likely was a tall tale.

New England Leftover Turkey Pie

"Crust":

1¼ cups stuffing mix

¼ cup melted butter

Filling:

½ cup milk

1 can (10½ oz.) condensed cream of celery soup

1½ cups leftover cooked turkey, cut in chunks

¾ cup frozen green peas

2 tblsps onion, minced

½ tsp salt

⅛ tsp coarsely ground black pepper

Topping:

¾ cup stuffing mix

¼ cup melted butter

Preheat oven to 425 degrees.

In a small bowl, mix together stuffing and butter. Press firmly into a 9-inch pie pan, covering sides and bottom. Using a saucepan, heat milk over low and gradually stir in soup until mixture is smooth. Add in the turkey, peas, onion, salt, and pepper. Set aside. In a separate bowl, combine ¾ cup stuffing with butter. Spoon filling into stuffing crust and sprinkle stuffing mix around top edges. Bake for about 10 minutes or until filling is bubbly. Serves 4 to 6.

The days of wagon trains brought about the basis for this recipe. Originally, it was made from lamb or wild game, as lambs could forage on sparse grasses and at times game was the only meat available. Beef chuck or stew meat will work fine.

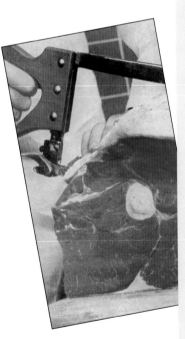

Oregon Trail's Best Pie

Filling:

½ cup all-purpose flour

1 tsps salt

¼ tsp coarsely ground black pepper

2 pounds lamb stew meat, beef chuck or stew chunks

¼ cup bacon drippings

3 cups water

1 tsp apple cider vinegar

½ tsp sugar

⅛ tsp ground cloves

1 bay leaf

3 carrots, peeled and sliced

1 onion, peeled and cut into thin wedges

3 potatoes, peeled and diced

2 tblsps all-purpose flour

3 tblsps water

Crust:

2 cups all-purpose flour

4 tsps baking powder

¼ tsp salt

¼ cup shortening (the pioneers used lard)

1¼ cups grated sharp cheddar cheese

⅔ cup milk

Preheat oven to 400 degrees.

To make the filling:

In a small bowl mix, together flour, salt, and pepper. Dredge meat in this and brown in drippings heated in a large heavy kettle. Add in water, vinegar, sugar, cloves, and bay leaf. Lower heat so mixture simmers gently, covered, for about 1½ hours. Meat should be tender. Add in carrots, onion, and potatoes, cover, and simmer another 20 to 25 minutes. Use a slotted spoon to remove meat and vegetables to a 2-quart baking dish. In a small container, blend together well the flour and 3 tablespoons water. Stir this into the remaining broth and stir until thickened. Pour over meat and vegetables.

To make the crust:

In a large bowl, sift together flour, baking powder, and salt. Blend in shortening with pastry cutter or your fingers until dough is crumbly. Stir in cheese. Mix in milk just until dough is moistened. Turn onto a floured board and knead three or four times. Roll dough into circle slightly larger than baking dish and seal over filling, crimping down edges and cutting vents for steam. Bake for 20 to 25 minutes until crust is light brown.

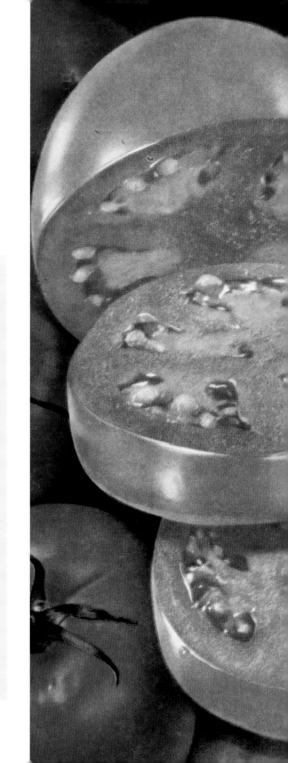

The word "tamale" originated as "tamalli" in the Aztec language. When the conquistadors arrived in Mexico City, known as Tenochtitlan to the Indians, they fell for the Aztec cuisine and took it back to Spain. Many Mexican dishes came to the country as Spanish when, in fact, they originated with the native Indians.

Southwest Tamale Pie

3 cups water

3½ tsps salt

1 cup yellow cornmeal

2 tblsps shortening

1 medium onion, chopped

1 small green bell pepper, chopped

1 pound ground chuck

½ tsp chile powder

4 medium tomatoes, sliced

1½ cups grated sharp cheddar cheese, or try one of the Mexican varieties.

In a large saucepan, bring the water to a boil with 1½ teaspoons salt, and slowly stir in cornmeal, stirring constantly. Continue cooking over low heat, stirring often, until thick, about 10 minutes. Remove from heat. Melt shortening in a large skillet and cook onion and green pepper over low heat until tender. Add in ground chuck and continue cooking until meat is browned. Stir in chile powder and remaining salt. Remove from heat. Preheat oven to 375 degrees. Spread half the cornmeal mixture on the bottom of a 8 x 13 x 2-inch baking dish. Cover this with meat mixture and sprinkle with half the cheese. Top with tomato slices. Repeat. Bake for 25 minutes, or until cheese is bubbly. Serves 4 to 6.

Simple Cheese Pie from Tillamook, Oregon

The Trask and Wilson Rivers wander through the lush wet forests of the Oregon Coast Range Mountains and onto a flood plain valley. Over many generations, this area has become loamy rich pastureland for thousands of dairy cattle. The result has been equally rich milk that travels every day to the world famous Tillamook Creamery. When my children were little visitors, they could watch the entire cheese making process, including workers hand cutting the enormous vats of curdled milk while the whey drained off. Nowadays, huge stainless steel machines do everything. The creamery is more "modern" with a gift shop, restaurant, and ice cream parlor. Tillamook makes much more than cheese now, but the quality of their most famous product is still outstanding.

Simple Cheese Pie

2 - 8 ounce packages cream cheese

¾ cup sugar

3 eggs

2 tsp vanilla extract

1 pint sour cream

1 - 8" graham cracker pie crust

Preheat oven to 300 degrees.

Cream cheese should be at room temperature. With your mixer, cream together the cream cheese with ½ cup of the sugar. Add in eggs, one at a time. Beat well. Add in 1 teaspoon of the vanilla. Pour into crust and bake for 45 minutes, or until firm. Cool for 20 minutes. With your mixer, beat together the remaining sugar and vanilla. Spread evenly over the cooled pie and refrigerate overnight. Serves 6 to 8.

Down Dixieland Way

Puffs, Crow's Nest, Jeff Davis, Stick-Tight, and No Matters are only a few of the charming names given to the pies of the south. Southern cooks have historically loaded down their tables with enough variety of rich foods to make the planks groan in protest, not the least of which are the choices of fine pies.

Digging among antique and secondhand stores for prizes, you may have come across what is known as a "pie safe" or "pie chest." Pies were kept in these small cupboards, usually with screen in the doors instead of wood or glass to keep the air circulating. Some say that Southerners corrupted the word into " 'ches" and thus came the name for a chess pie. Others claim that the South shouldn't get the blame because the word stems from the word cheese.

An old saying says one should eat Chess Pie in tiny slivers alongside a slice of white cake. This pie is superbly rich and the temptation to go back for more is a tough one to overcome.

Miz Lizzie's Chess Pie (Virginia)

½ cup sugar

4 tblsps real butter

3 eggs, separated

4 tblsps lemon juice

½ tsp lemon rind, grated

2 tsps stone-ground cornmeal

¼ tsp salt, divided in half

⅓ tsp cream of tartar

Pastry for 8-inch bottom crust
(See pages 8-9)

Preheat oven to 325 degrees.

In a medium bowl, cream together the sugar, butter, and beat until light and fluffy. Add in the egg yolks, lemon juice and rind, cornmeal and half the salt. In another bowl, beat the egg whites to soft peaks with the remaining salt and cream of tartar. Fold into butter mixture. Line pie pan with pastry, add in filling, and smooth over top. Bake on center rack until filling is firm, about 20 minutes. Serve at room temperature.

Fruit Pies

Muscadine Grapes are a prolific treasure of fencerows and thickets in southern states. Often living to a hundred years old, the hardy vines produce blue-green grapes with a strong musky flavor that makes a luscious pie. The darker blue-black version of this grape, that has the vintage name of Scuppernong, is used in a rich flavored local wine. Although he was a Pennsylvania boy, President James Buchanan loved the Muscadine grapes so much he ordered an arbor of them to be planted at the White House.

Schoolmarm's Strawberry Pie

Filling:

2 cups fresh strawberries, washed and sliced

¼ cup sugar

3 tblsps kirsch

1 pint (2 cups) whipping cream

¼ tsp salt

¼ cup sugar

6 egg yolks

1 tsp vanilla

1 cup brown sugar

Crust:

¼ cup butter

1 cup all-purpose flour

¼ tsp salt

2 tblsps milk

1 tblsp sugar

Preheat oven to 350 degrees.

In a medium bowl, blend together butter, flour, salt, milk, and sugar. The mixture should be crumbly. Press into a 9-inch pie pan and bake for about 30 minutes or until firm.

To make filling:
In a separate bowl, lightly toss the strawberries with sugar and kirsch. Set aside. In the top of a double boiler, scald the whipping cream and stir in salt and sugar. In a small bowl, beat together the egg yolks and stir into the cream. Cook over medium heat until mixture thickens. Remove from heat and stir in vanilla. Drain berries and spoon into baked pie crust. After egg mixture has cooled a little, pour over the berries. Chill well. Just before serving, sprinkle brown sugar over top of pie and place under broiler. Broil 5 minutes or until sugar melts and forms a top crust. Chill before serving. Serves 6 to 8.

The Pennsylvania Dutch are well known for their flavorful recipes and their pies are no exception. Schnitz is the regional word for dried apples and believe me, the difference between a Schnitz Pie and one from fresh apples is amazing. The filling for the former is more like applesauce, only with a more tart flavor and a rich butterscotch color. At the Pennsylvania Farm Museum, volunteers demonstrate how to "schnitz" apples using the pioneer method.

Schnitz Pie (Pennsylvania)

1 quart schnitz (dried, sliced sour apples, see page 43)
1 quart water
2 tblsps lemon juice
1 cup sugar
1 tblsp cornstarch
2 tblsps butter
Pastry for 2 crust 9-inch pie (See pages 8-9)

Preheat oven to 350 degrees.

Prepare the filling ahead of the crust so it has the chance to thicken up a little. In a large saucepan, simmer the schnitz with the water, covered, about 25 to 30 minutes until the apple slices are tender but not mushy. Add in the lemon juice. Mix about 2 tablespoons of sugar with the cornstarch, and then add to the apples along with the remaining sugar. Heat and stir the mixture until it thickens and turns clear, about 2 or 3 minutes. Remove from the heat and stir in butter. Cool to room temperature. Meanwhile, make the piecrust. Pour in the cooled filling and bake about 45 to 50 minutes until filling is bubbly and the crust is golden brown. Cool to room temperature before cutting.

How to Make Authentic Pennsylvania Dutch Schnitz

You'll need a good hard winter apple like McIntosh or Rhode Island Greening. Wash, pare, and slice about ⅛-inch thick. Place in a single layer on clean towels on cookie sheets and dry in your oven at 175 degrees. A food dryer is an easy alternative. The drying takes about 16 to 20 hours. Store in plastic bags in a cool, dry place, or in your freezer.

As American as (you guessed it)
Apple Pie

As early as the mid-1600s, a clergyman named William Blaxton planted some of the first apple orchards in New England. The apple he raised was the sweet Rhode Island Greening – the first apple recognized as strictly American.

In 1758 a Swedish minister wrote parishioners, "Apple-pie is used through the whole year, and when fresh apples are no longer to be had, dried ones are used. It is the evening meal of children. House-pie, in country homes, is made of apples neither peeled nor freed from their cores, and its crust is not broken if a wagon wheel goes over it."

Later in the mid-1800s a Midwestern immigrant wrote to his family in Scandinavia about a wonderful dish called "pai" made with apples, syrup and sugar.

The wonderful versatile apple has found a niché in almost every state with its very own adaptation of this famous pie.

Beacon Hill Apple Pie

**Pastry for 2-crust pie
(See pages 8-9)**

**4 large tart green apples (such as
Pippin or Granny Smith), peeled,
cored and sliced very thin**

1 cup sugar

¼ tsp salt

½ tsp ground cinnamon

½ tsp grated lemon rind

1 tblsp lemon juice

1 tblsp butter

2 tblsps cream

1 tblsp sugar

Preheat oven to 425 degrees.

Divide pastry in half and roll each piece in a circle. Line bottom of pie pan with pastry. Keep cool. In a medium bowl, toss together apple slices (there should be about 4 cups) with sugar, salt, cinnamon, lemon rind, and lemon juice. Pile apple mixture in pie pan. Dot with butter, seal on top crust, slash holes for steam, and bake for 10 minutes. Reduce heat to 350 degrees and continue baking 30 to 35 minutes. Five minutes before pie is done, brush top with cream and sprinkle with sugar. Serve warm with chunks of sharp cheddar cheese or vanilla ice cream. Serves 8.

An unknown cook said in the early 1800s every American family should find the space to plant their own orchard, especially with apples. She also forewarned that doing this would "preserve the orchard from the intrusion of boys, which is too common in America."

Hannibal, Mississippi, Apple Pie

3 cups homemade applesauce

Thin, flaky crust for double crust, 9-inch pie (See pages 8-9)

½ tsp ground cinnamon

Preheat oven to 450 degrees.

Pour applesauce into unbaked pie shell. Sprinkle with cinnamon. Top with second crust, seal and crimp edges. Bake for 20 minutes, then reduce heat to 375 and continue baking for 25 minutes longer. Crust should be golden brown. Serve warm with whipped cream.

WINESAP

YELLOW NEWTOWN

ROME BEAUTY

JONATHAN

Virginia Real Whiskey Apple Pie

2 cups tart green apples, peeled, cored, sliced (use Pippin, Cortland, Greening, or Granny Smith)

¼ cup water

1 cup light brown sugar, firmly packed

¼ cup (½ stick) butter

3 eggs, separated

¼ cup good bourbon whiskey

1 cup heavy cream

¼ tsp ground nutmeg

Pastry for single crust, 9-inch pie (See pages 8-9)

Preheat oven to 425 degrees.

In a saucepan, cook apple slices with water until tender. Beat with brown sugar and butter. Cool. Beat egg yolks until thick and lemon colored and stir into apple mixture. Stir in whiskey, cream, and nutmeg. In a separate bowl, beat egg whites to soft peaks and fold into apple mixture. Drizzle in a little more whiskey if desired. Line pie plate with pastry, pour in filling and bake 8 to 10 minutes. Reduce heat to 325 degrees and bake another 30 minutes. Filling should be set. Cool and serve with whipped cream. Serves 8.

Pink Kiss Rhubarb Pie

Pastry for a 2-crust pie (See pages 8-9)

3 cups ripe rhubarb, cut in ½-inch slices

1½ cups sugar

2 tblsps all-purpose flour

¼ tsp salt

1 tblsp lemon juice

2 egg yolks, slightly beaten

Preheat oven to 400 degrees.

Line a 9-inch pie tin with half of pastry. Line pastry with rhubarb. In a small bowl, mix together sugar, flour, salt, lemon juice, and egg yolks. Pour over the rhubarb and cover with top crust. Seal edges and make slashes in top for steam. Bake for 20 minutes then reduce heat to 350 degrees and continue baking about 20 minutes longer.

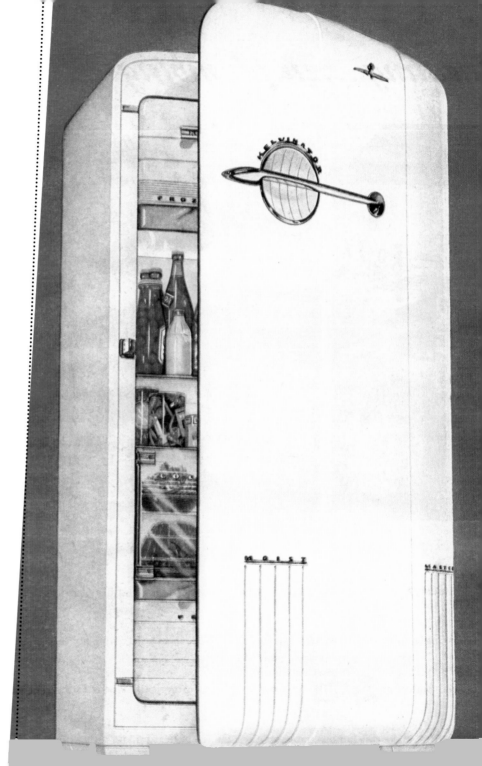

Rhubarb was a New World plant the early settler women renamed "pieplant" for obvious reasons. To this day, you will usually find a clump of rhubarb in most home gardens. The varieties are much improved now.

Alaskan Candied Rhubarb Pie

Filling:
5 cups rhubarb, diced
1 ¼ cups sugar
3 tblsps all-purpose flour
¼ tsp salt
2 tblsps butter, melted
1 egg, beaten
Pastry for single crust 9-inch pie
(See pages 8-9)

Topping:
½ cup sugar
½ cup all-purpose flour
⅛ tsp salt
¼ cup butter

Preheat oven to 425 degrees.

In a medium bowl, combine the rhubarb, 1¼ cups sugar, 3 tablespoons flour, ¼ teaspoon salt, 2 tablespoons butter, and egg. Pour into an unbaked pie shell. In a separate bowl, combine the ½ cup sugar, ½ cup flour, and ⅛ teaspoon salt. Cut in the ¼ cup butter until mixture is crumbly. Sprinkle this mixture over filling and bake for 40 minutes. If crust looks like it's getting too brown, turn down oven to 375 degrees.

The colonists picked the native grapes, known as "fox grapes," and used these as the foundation for what later became such rich descendants as the Concord. The Finger Lakes region of northwestern New York State has been serving this luscious Concord Grape pie for generations.

Early Autumn Grape Pie

5 cups fresh Concord Grapes (a kiss of early frost heightens the sugar content)

1 cup sugar

¼ cup all-purpose flour

2 tsps lemon juice

⅛ tsp salt

Pastry for 2-crust 9-inch pie* (See pages 8-9)

Preheat oven to 425 degrees.

Wash grapes and pinch out of skins. Save skins. Place pulp in a medium saucepan and bring to a boil. Cook 5 minutes or until pulp is tender. Press through a sieve to remove seeds. Mix pulp with reserved skins. Stir in sugar, flour, lemon juice, and salt. Spoon into pie shell, seal on top crust and cut steam vents. Bake 35 to 40 minutes.

*variation: Combine ½ cup quick-cooking oatmeal, ½ cup brown sugar, and ¼ cup flour. Blend in ¼ cup butter. Sprinkle over top of pie in place of top crust.

Impossibly Perfect Pear Pie

6 medium pears, peeled, cored, and sliced

¾ cup sugar

¼ cup all-purpose flour

¼ cup candied ginger, minced

3 tblsps lemon peel

2 tsps grated lemon juice

2 tblsps butter

Pastry for double-crust, 9-inch pie (See pages 8-9)

Preheat oven to 450 degrees.

Arrange pear slices in bottom crust. In a small bowl, combine sugar, flour, ginger, and lemon peel. Sprinkle over pear slices. Drizzle on the lemon juice and dot with butter. Seal on top crust and cut steam holes. Bake for 15 minutes. Reduce heat to 375 degrees and continue baking for another 40 minutes. Serves 8.

According to Martha Washington, the following was the recommended way to preserve cherries for pies and cobblers:

To keepe Cherries yt(so that) you may have them for tarts at Christmas without Preserving: Take ye fairest cherries you can get, fresh from ye trees, with out bruising, wipe them one by one with a linen cloth, yn (then) put ym (them) into a barrel of hay & lay them in ranks, first laying hay on the bottom, & then cherries & yn hay & yn cherries & then hay agayne, stop them close yt noe ayre get tp ym. Then set them under a fether bead where one layeth continually for ye warmer they are kept ye better it is soe they be neere no fire. Thus doeing you may have cherries any time of ye yeare. You allsoe May keep Cherries or other fruits, in glasses close stopt from ayre.

Here are a few cherry pie recipes handed down from the days of our first president:

Martha's Cherry Pie

4 cups tart pie cherries, pitted

3 tblsps quick-cooking tapioca

1¼ cups sugar

¼ tsp almond extract

1 tblsp lemon juice

**Pastry for 9-inch pie
(See pages 8-9)**

1½ tblsps butter

Preheat oven to 450 degrees.

In a medium bowl, mix together the cherries, tapioca, sugar, almond extract, and lemon juice. Let sit about 10 minutes. Line pie pan with bottom crust and spoon in cherry mixture. Dot with the butter and cover with top crust (a lattice crust is traditional). Bake for 10 minutes, reduce heat to 350 degrees. Continue baking for 40 to 45 minutes.

Amish Sour Cherry Pie

1 ¼ cups cherry juice

1 ½ cups water

⅛ tsp salt

⅔ cup sugar

5 tblsps quick-cooking tapioca

¼ tsp ground cinnamon

3 cups canned sour cherries, drained

Pastry for 2-crust, 9-inch pie (Bottom plus lattice top) (See pages 8-9)

In a medium saucepan, heat together cherry juice and 1 cup of the water. In a bowl, mix together the salt, sugar and tapioca with ½ cup water. Slowly stir this into the heated juice, stirring constantly. Cook until thick. Add cinnamon and cherries and stir. Chill. Preheat oven to 400 degrees. Pour cherry mixture into pie crust and top with a lattice crust. Bake for 10 to 15 minutes. Reduce heat to 350 degrees and bake until filling is bubbly and crust light brown, about 30 minutes. Serves 6 to 8.

Our first president has somehow been burdened with the charming, though false, story of chopping down a cherry tree. Washington probably never wielded the axe, but his name is often connected with cherry pie.

Heritage Orchard Traditional Cherry Pie

1 ½ cups sugar*

⅓ cup all-purpose flour

⅛ tsp salt

3 drops almond extract

4 cups pitted pie cherries

Pastry for 2-crust 9-inch pie (bottom plus lattice top) (See pages 8-9)

2 tblsps butter

Preheat oven to 425 degrees.

In a medium bowl, combine sugar, flour, and salt. Toss almond extract with cherries, then the sugar mixture. Spoon into the unbaked pie shell and dot with butter. Place lattice top and bake approximately 40 minutes. Watch so crust doesn't burn. If necessary, cover edge with foil. Serves 6 to 8.

*Reduce sugar to 1 ⅓ cup if you like a more tart pie.

Sweet Spring Cherry Pie

Pastry for single-crust, 9-inch pie (See pages 8-9)

2 (1 pound) cans pitted, dark sweet cherries

⅔ cup sugar

3 tblsps cornstarch

⅛ tsp salt

1 tblsp butter

2 tblsps lemon juice

1 (3 oz.) package cream cheese, softened

Preheat oven to 350 degrees.

Bake pie shell until light golden brown. Cool. Drain cherries. Save juice. In a medium saucepan, combine sugar, cornstarch, and salt. Add 1 cup of the cherry juice. Cook over medium heat, stirring constantly, until mixture comes to a boil. Cook for about 2 minutes. Add cherries and cook another 2 minutes. Remove from heat and stir in butter and lemon juice, stirring until butter melts. Cool. Spread softened cream cheese over bottom of baked pie shell and pour over cherry mixture. Chill at least 3 hours. Serve with whipped cream (optional). Serves 6 to 8.

Deep Dish Plum Pie

1 cup sugar

¼ tsp ground cinnamon

¼ cup all-purpose flour

2½ pounds (approximately 3 – 3½ cups) firm sweet plums, halved and pitted

Pastry for single crust, 9-inch pie (See pages 8-9)

2 ½ tblsps butter

2 tblsps milk

1 tsp sugar

Preheat oven to 425 degrees.

In a medium bowl, combine sugar, cinnamon, and flour. Toss with plums. Place in deep pie dish lined with pastry. Dot with butter. Seal top crust and cut slashes for steam. Brush top with milk. Bake for 45 to 50 minutes. Should be golden brown. Sprinkle top with sugar. Serve with a dollop of vanilla ice cream. Serves 6 to 8.

This recipe is a county fair blue-ribbon winner from a Kansas farm wife. Although modernized a bit, the basic flavor is still delectable and rich.

Across the country gnarled, scraggly wild plum trees can be seen, often along with ancient apple and pear trees, the only lasting evidence of where a homestead once stood. Plums, including the Italian Prune Plum, have been a part of country life since the early pioneers traveled from the barely civilized eastern United States to what was then called "the West": Ohio, Kentucky, Indiana, and Tennessee.

Rogue Valley Streusel Pear Pie

½ cup sugar

1½ tblsps quick-cooking tapioca

⅛ tsp ground mace

½ tsp ground cinnamon

2 tblsps lemon juice

6 cups firm ripe pears, pared and sliced (I like Bosc, D'Anjou, or Bartlett)

½ cup butter

1 cup flour

1 cup brown sugar, firmly packed

Unbaked 9-inch pie crust (See pages 8-9)

Preheat oven to 375 degrees.

In a large bowl, combine sugar, tapioca, mace, and cinnamon. Stir in lemon juice and pears. Let sit for 15 minutes. Meanwhile, cut butter into flour and brown sugar until crumbly. Spoon pear mixture into pie crust and sprinkle crumb mixture over top. Bake for 45 to 50 minutes or until golden brown. Serve with a scoop of vanilla ice cream. Serves 6 to 8.

For nearly ten years, I lived in the Rogue Valley in Oregon, a place famous for its wonderful fruit, especially pears. This recipe was brought over the Oregon Trail, down the Willamette Valley, and into the southern corner of the state by hardy pioneers.

President Buchanan's Grape Pie (North Carolina)

Pastry for 9-inch bottom crust plus enough pastry for lattice top

4 cups Muscadine grapes (if unavailable, substitute any blue slip-skin variety such as Concord), washed, stems removed

1 cup sugar

1/8 tsp salt

1 tblsp orange juice

1 tblsp lemon juice

1 tsp orange rind, grated

1 tsp lemon rind, grated

1 tblsp quick-cooking tapioca

Preheat oven to 450 degrees.

Line pie pan with bottom crust. Slip skins from grapes and set aside. Cook grape pulp for a few minutes until the seeds loosen. Press pulp through a colander. In a medium bowl, mix pulp, skins, sugar, salt, orange and lemon juice, orange and lemon rind, and tapioca. Turn into pastry shell and top with lattice strips. Bake in the hot, 450 degree oven for 10 minutes. Turn down heat to 350 degrees and bake until juice bubbles and crust is brown, about 25 minutes more.

Red Brick Café's Banana Cream Pie

²⁄₃ **cup sugar**

3½ tblsps cornstarch

½ tsp salt

2½ cups milk

3 egg yolks, slightly beaten

1 tsp vanilla

2 large bananas, sliced

Pastry for single crust 9-inch pie, baked (See pages 8-9)

Meringue (See page 91)

In the top of a double boiler, combine sugar, cornstarch, and salt. Stir in the milk and cook over medium heat until mixture thickens, stirring constantly. Cover and continue cooking another 15 minutes. Spoon about ¼ cup of this hot mixture into the beaten egg yolks, then stir back into the hot pudding. Cook another 2 minutes. Cool. Add in vanilla. Slice bananas into the baked crust, arranging neatly around. Pour filling over top. Top with meringue and brown according to directions on page 91. Serves 6-8.

China gets the praise and recognition as the birthplace of the wonderful peach. But, for generations America has thought of this fine fruit as southern, more specifically from Georgia. In truth, peaches are grown all across the country where everywhere the scent of peach jam, canned peaches, cobblers, and pie sweeten the summer air.

This recipe is an adaptation of an old Georgia open-face pie:

Meriwether County Glazed Peach Pie

6 cups firm ripe peaches, pared and sliced

1 cup sugar

3 tblsps cornstarch

¼ tsp ground cinnamon

½ cup orange juice

9-inch pie crust (See pages 8-9)

Preheat oven to 375 degrees and bake pie crust for 15 minutes, or until lightly browned.

In a medium bowl, mash enough peaches to make 1 cup. Set aside remaining sliced peaches. In a small saucepan, combine sugar, cornstarch, and cinnamon. Stir in orange juice and mashed peaches. Cook over medium heat until mixture comes to a boil, stirring occasionally. Continue boiling for 1 minute longer. Spread half of this glaze over the sides and bottom of the baked crust. Fill with peach slices and pour remaining glaze over all. Chill in refrigerator at least 3 hours. Serve with whipped cream. Serves 8.

The Long Beach Peninsula in Washington State, where I live, has many acres of cranberry bogs. Not only are cranberry recipes plentiful, there is a long historical use of this tart bright red fruit. We locals like to imagine the famed Lewis and Clark expedition being shown how to make pemmican out of pounded game meats and native berries. Now, with the improved varieties of cranberries, the recipes multiply every year. However, this is an old time recipe whose origin has been lost.

Peninsula Surprise Pie

1 cup raw cranberries, washed and sorted, frozen are okay

5½ cups apples, peeled, cored, sliced (I like a variety with a little snap, like McIntosh, Fuji, Pink Lady, or Braeburn)

¼ cup canned, crushed pineapple in its own syrup, drained

½ cup brown sugar, firmly packed

¼ cup white sugar

1 tsp grated orange peel

½ tsp ground cinnamon

¼ tsp ground nutmeg

Pastry for double crust 9-inch pie (See pages 8-9)

Preheat oven to 400 degrees.

In your food processor or grinder, combine cranberries, ½ cup apple slices, pineapple, brown sugar, white sugar, orange peel, cinnamon, and nutmeg. Process until well chopped, but not mushy. Spread half of this mixture on bottom of pie crust. Arrange apple slices over this and cover with remaining cranberry mixture. Top with remaining crust, sealing edges well and cutting steam vents. Bake for 15 minutes then reduce heat to 350 degrees and bake for an additional 35 to 40 minutes. You might have to cover crust edge with aluminum foil to prevent it from burning. Serves 6 to 8.

Until the 1830s the lowly blackberry vine and its fruit were thought of as little more than a pesky weed. Here and there, there was a recipe to use the blackberry fruit as a medicinal syrup for "cholera and summer complaint." Somehow, the vine made its way to the west coast. We here in the Pacific Northwest have a love/hate relationship with this plant. On the one hand, the vines seem to be indestructible, taking over yards, hillsides, even buildings like the Kudzu does in the south. However, summertime brings out brave souls who pick the luscious blue/black berries roadside, their arms battle scarred from the thorns, clothes tattered, smiles tinged with purple, and buckets brimming with succulent fruit for jams, cobblers, "slumps," roly-polys, and fine pies.

Applegate River Blackberry Pie

4 cups fresh blackberries, washed and sorted

3 tblsps flour

1 cup sugar

1 tblsp lemon juice

¼ tsp ground cinnamon

Pastry for a 2-crust 9-inch pie (See pages 8-9)

1 tblsp butter

Preheat oven to 450 degrees.

In a medium bowl, gently toss the berries with flour, sugar, lemon juice, and cinnamon. Line a pie pan with half of the pastry and spoon in berry mixture. Dot with the butter. Cover with top crust, cutting a few slashes for steam. Bake for 15 minutes then reduce heat to 350 degrees and bake an additional 35 to 40 minutes. Serves 6 to 8.

Alaskan Wild Berry Pie

2 cups blueberries, huckleberries, or similar fruit; washed and sorted

1 cup sugar

½ tsp lemon juice

⅛ tsp nutmeg

3 tblsps all-purpose flour

1 cup blueberries (or whatever you're using), washed and sorted

Pastry for double, 9-inch pie crust (See pages 8-9)

1 tblsp all-purpose flour

Preheat oven to 425 degrees.

In a medium bowl, combine the 2 cups berries with sugar, lemon juice, and nutmeg. Toss gently to avoid smashing berries. Stir in flour. Turn into a saucepan and cook on low just until mixtures bubbles. Remove from heat. Cool. Sprinkle the single tablespoon of flour over the bottom of the crust and cover with the cup of raw berries. Pour cooked filling over raw berries and top with crust; cutting a few steam vents. Place on a cookie sheet and bake for 10 minutes. Reduce heat to 350 and continue cooking until crust is lightly browned and filling is bubbly. Serves 6 to 8.

Pennsylvania Dutch Raisin Pie

Pastry for 9-inch, single crust pie (See pages 8-9)
1 cup sugar
1½ tblsps cornstarch
½ tsp ground cinnamon
¼ tsp ground nutmeg
¼ tsp ground allspice
¼ tsp salt
1½ cups sour cream
3 eggs, separated
1½ cups raisins
1 tblsp lemon juice
¼ tsp cream of tartar
6 tblsps sugar (again)
½ tsp vanilla
Meringue (See page 91)

In colonial America, fresh fruit was available for only a few months of the year. However, raisins and other dried fruit were brought out for mid-winter treats such as the following yummy pie. Legend has it this pie was originally called "Funeral Pie" as it was served at the huge meals following a family funeral gathering. In fact, when someone was seriously ill, the saying "There will be a raisin pie soon" foretold doom. Nowadays, this delightful dessert is seen commonly at country tables without the dismal connection.

Line pie pan with pastry and bake according to directions on page 72. In a medium saucepan, combine together sugar, cornstarch, cinnamon, nutmeg, allspice, and salt. Blend in sour cream. In a separate bowl, beat eggs slightly and stir into sour cream mixture. Add in raisins and lemon juice. Cook over medium heat, stirring constantly, until mixture comes to a boil and thickens. Boil 1 minute. Pour into baked pie shell. Beat egg whites until frothy with cream of tartar. Beat in the 6 tablespoons sugar, one tablespoonful at a time, until mixture is shiny and it forms stiff peaks. Beat in vanilla. Spread meringue over hot filling making sure to seal up to the edges. Serves 6 to 8.

APPLE

CHERRY

BANANA

You can make <u>any kind of pie</u>

easily, quickly, perfectly—

BLUEBERRY

Turn-of-the-Century Apricot or Prune Pie

Pastry for single crust, 9-inch pie

¾ cup apricot puree (or prune)

½ tsp grated lemon rind

1 tblsp lemon juice

3 egg whites

⅛ tsp salt

½ cup sugar

1 cup heavy cream, whipped

Preheat oven to 450 degrees.

Line pie pan with pastry, crimp edges, and bake for about 15 minutes. Crust should be light golden brown. Cool. In a medium bowl, combine apricot (or prune) puree. Make the puree by running drained canned apricots in your blender or food processor. To ¾ cup of the puree, add lemon rind and juice. In a separate bowl, beat the egg whites until stiff. Beat in salt and gradually add the sugar. Fold this into the fruit puree and spoon into baked pie crust. Bake at 325 for about 20 minutes. Serve with whipped cream. Serves 6 to 8.

Shoo-Fly Pie

The well known Southern delight Shoo-Fly Pie has almost as many variations as apple pie. Some like to dunk their bites of Shoo-Fly and prefer it dry. Others ask for the "wet bottom" style. Molasses is the key ingredient in every version.

Crumb Mixture:
1 ½ cups all-purpose flour
½ cup brown sugar, firmly packed
⅛ tsp salt
⅛ tsp ground ginger
⅛ tsp ground nutmeg
½ tsp ground cinnamon
¼ cup butter, slightly softened

Filling:
½ tsp baking soda
½ cup molasses
⅔ cup of the crumb mixture

**Pastry for a 1-crust pie
(See pages 8-9)**

Preheat oven to 375 degrees.

To make mixture:
Line an 8-inch pie pan with pastry. Refrigerate while you prepare the rest. In a medium bowl combine flour, brown sugar, salt, ginger, nutmeg, and cinnamon. Blend in the butter until the mixture is like coarse meal. Set aside.

To make filling:
In a saucepan, pour in boiling water and stir in baking soda and molasses. Add in the ⅔ crumb mixture and pour into chilled pie shell. Bake for 30 to 40 minutes or until crust and crumbs are a nice golden brown.

Washington Irving's Mincemeat Pie

2 pounds lean ground beef

1 pound ground suet
   (you can get this from your butcher)

2 pounds sugar

5 pounds tart cooking apples,
   pared, cored and chopped

1 pound currants

1 pound raisins

½ pound citron, chopped

½ pound orange peel, chopped

Brandy (optional)

Pastry for a 2-crust pie (See pages 8-9)

1 tsp salt

1 tsp cinnamon

1 tsp mace

1 tsp allspice

1 quart cider (approximate)

Although this recipe is written in the old form (by the pound), it's well worth the extra time and trouble.

To make filling:
In a large canning kettle, mix together beef, suet, sugar, apples, currants, raisins, citron, orange peel, salt, cinnamon, mace, allspice, and cider. Simmer over low heat, covered, for 2 hours. Stir often. If mixture becomes too dry add in cider a little at a time. Mincemeat should be moist but not sloppy. Stir in a few tablespoons brandy to taste.

To make the pie:
Preheat oven to 450 degrees.

Line a 9-inch pie pan with the pastry and spoon in mincemeat. Do not overfill. Cover with a thin crust, seal well and cut in a few places for steam to escape. Bake for 30 minutes. Should be served warm. Or, pack mincemeat into hot sterilized 1-pint, or 1-quart, canning jars and process in pressure cooker 20 minutes at 10 pounds pressure.

Country Bridge Mincemeat Pie

This is a turn of the century Mennonite recipe

2 cups lean beef or venison, cooked, ground
3 cups tart apples, peeled, cored, finely chopped
½ cup dark brown sugar, packed
½ tsp ground cloves
1 tsp ground cinnamon
½ tsp salt
3 tblsps whiskey
4 tblsps black cherry wine
¼ cup raisins
Pastry for 2-crust, 9-inch pie (See pages 8-9)

Preheat oven to 350 degrees.

In a medium saucepan, combine beef, apples, brown sugar, cloves, cinnamon, and salt. Cook over low until thoroughly heated. Stir in whiskey, wine, and raisins. Spoon into pie shell and cover with top crust. Seal edges well. Make a few slashes in top for steam. Bake for 45 minutes. Serve hot. Serves 8.

Mock Mincemeat Pie

1 cup raisins

1 cup hot water

1 cup apples, peeled and chopped

2 cups sugar

1 cup bread cubes

1½ tblsp apple cider vinegar

1 egg, beaten

¼ cup butter, softened

1½ tsps ground cinnamon

½ tsp ground nutmeg

Pastry for double crust, 9-inch pie (See pages 8-9)

Preheat oven to 450 degrees.

Soak raisins in the hot water for a few minutes to soften. Drain. In a bowl, toss together apples, raisins, sugar, bread cubes, egg, butter, cinnamon, and nutmeg. Into a 1 cup measuring cup, measure in vinegar and add enough water to make a full cup. Pour this over apple mixture. Spoon this into a deep dish pie plate lined with pastry. Seal on top crust and cut steam vents. Bake for 15 minutes, then reduce heat to 350 degrees and continue baking for another 45 minutes, or until lightly brown. Offer your favorite topping of whipped cream, ice cream, or sharp cheese. Serves 8.

Floridian Macaroon Pie

6 tblsp butter, melted

1⅓ cups sugar

2 tblsps all-purpose flour

3 eggs

1 (12-ounce) can evaporated milk

1 (3½ ounce) can coconut (about 1 cup)

1 tsp vanilla

Pastry for single crust 9-inch pie (See pages 8-9)

Preheat oven to 350 degrees.

In a bowl, mix together the butter, sugar, and flour. Add in eggs, canned milk, coconut, and vanilla. Mix well. Pour into pie crust and bake for 35 to 40 minutes, or until filling is set and firm. Serves 8 (this is a rich pie!).

Homesteader's Oatmeal Pie (Oklahoma)

2 eggs, slightly beaten

⅔ cup butter, melted and cooled

⅔ cup sugar

⅔ cup leftover cooked oatmeal (I prefer thick cut)

⅔ cup white Karo syrup (you can use the dark variety or light molasses for a more historical taste)

1 tsp vanilla

Pastry for 9-inch pie (See pages 8-9)

Preheat oven to 350 degrees.

In a medium bowl mix, together the eggs, butter, sugar, oatmeal, Karo, and vanilla. Pour into the pastry shell and bake for 50 minutes. Serves 8.

In 1831, Kentucky State senator Robert Wickliffe commented, "Let a stranger visit your country and enquire for your best specimens of agriculture, mechanics and architecture, and sir, he is directed to visit the Society of Shakers." Even then, the Kentuckians knew the food from Shaker colonies was the absolute finest in the South.

Shaker Hill Pecan Pie

3 eggs, slightly beaten

1 cup light corn syrup

1 cup light brown sugar, packed

⅓ cup melted butter

⅛ tsp salt

1 tsp vanilla

1 cup pecans, halves or broken

Pastry for single-crust, 9-inch pie
   (See pages 8-9)

Preheat oven to 350 degrees.

In a medium bowl, beat together eggs, corn syrup, brown sugar, butter, salt, and vanilla. Fold in pecans and pour into unbaked pie shell. Bake about 1 hour. Crust should be golden brown and filling should be the consistency of jelly. Pie will set further as it cools. Cool to room temperature before cutting or pie will run. This is a very rich pie, so cut in small slices. Serves 8 to 10.

Early settlers to the south found the tall pecan and hickory trees growing wild and loaded with nuts. Native Americans called the nuts pegans, which meant hard shell. They pounded the nuts into meal for small cakes and other dishes, rinsing the pecan meal multiple times to rid it of the bitter tannin.

The bitter tannin and the tough shell have been bred out of the present day pecan, which is cultivated in Florida, Georgia, and west Texas.

Legend says that the pride of the south pie derived from the English chess pie recipe. Cane syrup and molasses were the original sweeteners whereas light corn syrup is used today.

Chattahooche County Pecan Pie

3 eggs
2/3 cup sugar
1/8 tsp salt
1 cup dark corn syrup
1/4 cup + 2 tblsps butter, melted
1 cup pecan halves or pieces
Unbaked 9-inch pie crust
  (See pages 8-9)

Preheat oven to 350 degrees.

In a large mixing bowl, beat eggs well. Add in sugar, salt, corn syrup and butter. Mix well. Add pecans. Pour into pie shell and bake for 50 minutes or until knife inserted halfway between center and edge comes out clean. Cool before cutting. Serves 8.

Deep South Peanut Butter Pie

1½ cups blanched, shelled raw peanuts

1 cup molasses, light, sorghum, or dark corn syrup

½ cup sugar

½ cup (1 stick) butter

4 eggs

1 tsp vanilla

⅛ tsp salt

¼ tsp ground nutmeg

Pastry for single-crust, 9-inch pie

Preheat oven to 325 degrees.

Spread peanuts out on a baking sheet and "parch" (roast) for about 40 to 45 minutes. Cool. Grind in food processor. Pack into a measuring cup to make 1 cup. In a medium bowl, mix together peanuts, molasses, sugar, butter, eggs, vanilla, salt, and nutmeg. Turn oven up to 375 degrees. Pour filling into pie shell and bake for 35 minutes or until crust is light brown. Cool to room temperature before cutting. Serves 6.

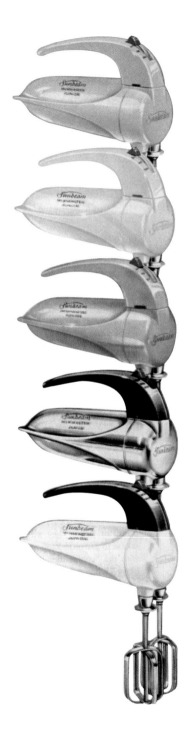

Great Aunt Eleanor's Maple-Nut Pie

3 eggs

¾ cup sugar

¾ cup real Vermont Maple Syrup (no substitutes!)

3 tblsps melted butter

⅛ tsp salt

1 tblsp apple cider vinegar

1¼ cup pecans, chopped

Pastry for single 9-inch crust (See pages 8-9)

Preheat oven to 450 degrees.

Beat the eggs well, gradually adding in sugar. Mix in maple syrup, butter, salt, and vinegar. Stir in pecans and pour into unbaked pie crust. Bake for 10 minutes then reduce heat to 350 degrees (do not open oven door) and continue baking for 30 to 35 minutes or until set. Cool. Serves 8.

Texarkana, Texas Praline Pie

This fine rich pie is often the finale to a meal of freshly caught deep fried catfish and hush puppies.

3 egg whites

½ tsp baking powder

1 cup sugar

1 tsp vanilla

20 butter crackers (like Keebler's), crushed

¾ cup pecans, chopped

Preheat oven to 425 degrees.

With your mixer, beat together egg whites, baking powder, and vanilla until stiff. Gradually add in sugar a tablespoon at a time. Fold in cracker crumbs and pecans. Pour into a well-greased pie pan. Bake for 30 minutes. Cool. Top with whipped cream. Serves 8 to 10.

Family Reunion Walnut Pie

3 tblsps all-purpose flour

½ cup water

1 cup sugar

2 eggs, beaten

¾ cup light molasses

1½ cups milk

1½ cups walnuts, chopped

**Pastry for two 8-inch pie shells
  (See pages 8-9)**

In a saucepan, combine flour and water to make a smooth paste. Add in sugar, eggs, molasses, and milk. Cook over medium heat, stirring constantly, until mixture is very thick. Remove from heat and cool. Stir in walnuts and pour into baked pie shells. Chill for several hours before slicing. Serves 6 to 8.

Pope's Ferry Inn Chocolate/Peanut Pie

2 squares unsweetened baking chocolate

¼ cup butter

¼ cup brown sugar, firmly packed

¾ cup white sugar

½ cup milk

¼ cup light corn syrup

1½ tsps vanilla

3 eggs

1 cup salted peanuts, coarsely chopped

Unbaked 9-inch pie crust (See pages 8-9)

There's a myth that peanuts (a.k.a. "goobers") originated in Brazil. The real story is credited to the pre-Incan Peruvians who called them "ground seeds" and offered them as provisions to help the spirit of the dead on its way, assuming to sun god heaven. This recipe may not get you to heaven, but the taste is definitely heavenly. Of course, this is a southern recipe.

Preheat oven to 350 degrees.

In the top of a double boiler, melt together the chocolate and butter, stirring occasionally. Remove from heat and cool slightly. In a mixing bowl, combine brown sugar, white sugar, milk, corn syrup, vanilla and eggs. Beat well with mixer. Beat in chocolate mixture. Stir in peanuts and pour into pie crust. Bake for 45 to 50 minutes or until knife inserted in center comes out clean. Cool thoroughly before cutting. Serves 8.

* The filling cooks up in layers with the crunchy peanuts on the top.

Savannah Anna's Pumpkin Pie

1 (8 oz.) package cream cheese, room temperature
¾ cup brown sugar, firmly packed
1 tsp ground cinnamon
½ tsp salt
½ tsp ground ginger
¼ tsp ground cloves
3 eggs
1 cup canned pumpkin
1 cup milk
1 tsp vanilla
Unbaked 9-inch pie crust
  (See pages 8-9)
1 cup sour cream
2 tblsps sugar

Preheat oven to 375 degrees.

In a large mixing bowl, cream together the cream cheese, brown sugar, cinnamon, salt, ginger, and cloves. Add eggs, one at a time, beating after each one. Mix in pumpkin, milk, and vanilla. Pour into pie crust and bake for 45 to 50 minutes. Check center with a clean butter knife. In a small bowl, blend together sour cream and sugar. Spread over top of pie and return to oven for 3 to 5 minutes. Chill before serving. Serves 6 to 8.

Most school children have heard the story of how pumpkins and squash were introduced to the early American colonists. The Native Americans in New England considered the pumpkin as critical to their diet as corn (maize) and beans. And this history continues on far south to Peru where pre-Incan people grew the lowly pumpkin and painted pictures of it on their pottery.

European transplants get the credit for taking this native vegetable and making it into a delectable holiday pie.

The recipe on this page has several twists, but the flavor is still rich and delightful.

Sunbeam
MIXMASTER

PINK   YELLOW

TURQUOISE   CHROME

Custard Pies

The Absolutely Perfect Meringue!

*For one 8-inch pie

3 egg whites, room temperature
⅛ tsp salt
¼ tsp cream of tartar
6 tblsps sugar

Preheat oven to 350 degrees.

In a small deep bowl on your electric mixer, beat egg whites with salt and cream of tartar at high speed until soft peaks form. Whip in 2 tablespoons of sugar at a time until egg whites form stiff peaks. Sugar should be dissolved. Spoon meringue onto your cooled pie filling and make certain meringue seals with crust to prevent "weeping." Use the back of a spoon to make swirls. Bake for 12 to 15 minutes until meringue is lightly brown. Cool away from drafts.

Abe Lincoln's Favorite Lemon Pie

Filling:
1 cup sugar
1 tblsp cornstarch
⅛ tsp salt
1 tblsp grated lemon rind
¼ cup fresh lemon juice
⅔ cup water
4 egg yolks
1 egg
2 tblsps melted butter

Meringue:
4 egg whites
3 tblsps sugar

**Pastry for single-crust 8-inch pie
(See pages 8-9)**

Preheat oven to 325 degrees.

To make filling:
In a medium bowl, combine sugar, cornstarch, and salt. Add in lemon rind, juice, and water. Beat in egg yolks, one at a time, leaving the whole egg until last. Blend in melted butter. Pour into unbaked pie shell and bake for 30 to 35 minutes until bubbly and somewhat thick. Remove from oven and let sit for 10 minutes. Heat oven to 450 degrees.

To make meringue:
Beat egg whites until frothy. Beat in sugar, a little at a time, until whites form soft peaks. Spread over pie, making sure to seal edges. Bake 2 to 3 minutes until meringue is lightly touched with brown. Cool to room temperature before cutting.
Serves 6 to 8.

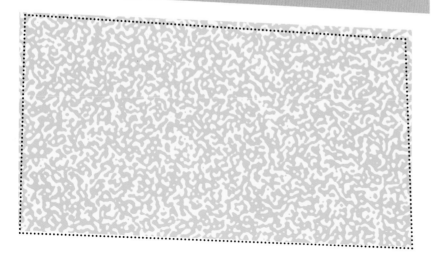

After Abe Lincoln was elected to the Illinois Legislature in 1834 (he served four two-year terms), he spent many days traveling around the state to visit his constituents. Mrs. Nancy Breedlove owned one small hotel where the future president stayed. She served a delectable tart lemon custard pie. Lincoln so enjoyed this pie he asked for the recipe and took it with him to the White House.

Boone's Kentucky Tavern Lemon Pie

5 eggs
1½ cups light corn syrup
¼ cup fresh lemon juice
1 tblsp grated lemon rind
¼ cup butter
Pastry for single crust 9-inch pie

Preheat oven to 375 degrees.

In a medium mixing bowl, beat together the eggs and add in syrup. Mix in lemon juice, and rind. Beat well. Add in butter and beat until mixed in. Pour into unbaked pie crust and place on bottom shelf of oven. Bake for 10 minutes; move to the middle shelf and reduce heat to 350. Continue baking for another 30 to 40 minutes. Serves 6.

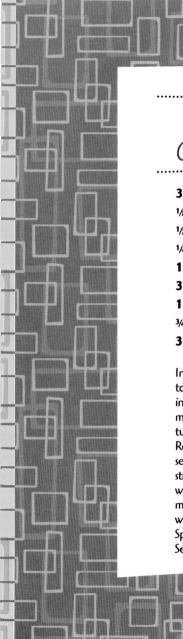

Aunt Mable's
Connecticut Lemon Pie

3 egg yolks
⅛ tsp salt
½ cup sugar
¼ cup fresh lemon juice
1 tsp grated lemon rind
3 egg whites
1 cup whipping cream
¾ cup vanilla wafers, crushed
3 tblsps melted butter

In the top of a double boiler, beat together egg yolks, salt and sugar. Stir in lemon juice and rind. Cook over medium high heat until mixture turns thick. It should coat a spoon. Remove from heat and chill. In a separate bowl, beat egg whites until stiff. Whip cream. Fold egg whites and whipped cream into chilled cooked mixture. Mix together crushed wafers with butter and press into a pie pan. Spoon in filling and freeze until firm. Serves 6 to 8.

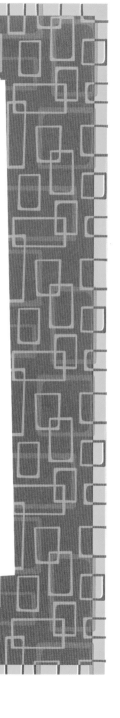

Traveling across the prairies in the mid 1800s, the pioneer women had few amenities. But they always made sure there was plenty of homemade vinegar. This trusty and potent solution was used for everything from pot scrubbing to pickling, sanitizing to sore throats, shining mirrors to tenderizing that tough roast from an ancient cow. Lemons were a seldom-seen luxury but that never slowed down the resourceful Nebraskan pioneer woman.

Webster County Vinegar Pie (Nebraska)

1 cup sugar
3 tblsps all-purpose flour
¼ tsp ground mace
¾ cup water
3 tblsps apple cider vinegar
⅓ cup butter, melted
2 large eggs, lightly beaten
Pastry for 8-inch pie
(See pages 8-9)

Preheat oven to 350 degrees.

In a medium bowl blend together sugar, flour, and mace. Stir in water, vinegar, butter, and eggs and beat just enough to mix. Pour mixture into unbaked pie shell and bake for 50 to 55 minutes. Filling should be puffy and lightly browned. Cool to room temperature before cutting. Filling will fall slightly and thicken to a custard-like consistency. Serves 8.

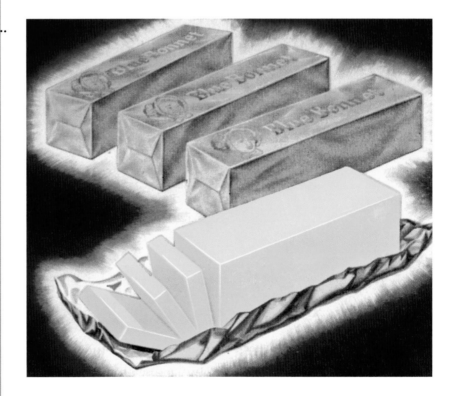

This recipe has been in an Oklahoma family for more than 100 years. A tradition at reunions and holidays, this pie is also a blue ribbon winner at many county fairs.

Land Rush Molasses Pie

4 eggs, separated
1 cup sugar
½ cup light corn syrup
½ cup light molasses
1 tblsp all-purpose flour
2 cups milk
¼ tsp ground cinnamon
1½ cups pecans or walnuts, chopped
Pastry for 2 single crust 9-inch pies (See pages 8-9)

Preheat oven to 350 degrees.

Beat egg yolks in a medium bowl. Stir in sugar, corn syrup, molasses, andflour. Beat well. Gradually stir in milk and cinnamon. In a separate bowl, beat egg whites until stiff. Gently fold whites into molasses mixture. Spoon into two unbaked pie crusts and sprinkle with nuts. Bake for 50 minutes or until filling is firm. Cool before serving. Top with whipped cream. Each pie serves 6 to 8.

Pineapple Cream Pie from the Colonial Inn

3 tblsps flour

1 cup sugar

2 egg yolks

2 cups milk

1 tblsp butter

1 cup pineapple (canned is okay, but fresh is definitely better!), cubed

Pastry for single crust 9-inch pie, baked (See pages 8-9)

Meringue (See page 91)

In the top of a double boiler, combine flour and sugar. Mix in egg yolks and milk with a wire whip. Cook over medium heat until mixture thickens. Stir in butter and pineapple. Pour into baked pie crust and cover with meringue. Serves 6.

Front Porch Sweet Cheese Pie

Crust:

2 cups zwieback crackers (or other similar plain crackers), crushed

¼ cup butter, melted

⅛ tsp ground cinnamon

Filling:

1 package, (8 oz.) cream cheese, softened

½ cup sugar

2 eggs

½ tsp vanilla

Topping:

1 cup sour cream

2 tblsps sugar

½ tsp vanilla

To make crust:

In a medium bowl, mix together crushed crackers, butter, and cinnamon. Press into a 9-inch pie pan or similar baking dish. Chill.

To make filling:

In a medium bowl, beat together cream cheese, sugar, eggs, and vanilla. Pour into pie crust and bake at 375 degrees for 20 minutes. Cool.

To make topping:

In a small bowl, beat together sour cream, sugar, and vanilla. Spread this over cooled pie and bake at 475 degrees for exactly 5 minutes. Chill before serving. Serves 6 to 8.

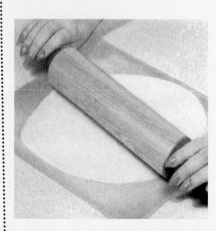

There are still grange halls active across the country where the ladies (and often now the gents) bring their prized pies and other fine dishes for charities and potlucks. The grange has been the backbone for American farmers since 1867, providing political, social, and economic support. Although the recipes on these two pages and the following two pages have evolved over the years, they still deserve honor among the grange favorites.

Grange Apple-Custard Pie

**Pastry for single crust, 9-inch pie
(See pages 8-9)**

1 tblsp butter

²/₃ cup sugar

¹/₈ tsp ground cinnamon

2 eggs, well beaten

¹/₂ cup heavy cream

**2¹/₂ cups cooked apple slices
(canned is okay)**

Preheat oven to 450 degrees.

Line pie pan with pastry. In a medium bowl, combine butter, sugar, cinnamon, eggs, and cream. Stir until smooth. Add in apples. Spoon into pastry and bake for 10 minutes. Reduce heat to 350 degrees and continue baking for 20 to 25 minutes. Filling should be set. Chill before serving. Serves 6 to 8.

Grange Blue-Ribbon Caramel Pie

½ pound (about 28) caramel candies

1 cup milk

⅛ tsp salt

1 envelope (1 tblsp) unflavored gelatin

¼ cup cold water

1 cup heavy cream, whipped

½ cup pecans, chopped

1 tsp vanilla

Single crust gingersnap crust (see recipe on page 9 for graham cracker crust)

In the top of a double boiler, melt the caramels over boiling water, stirring occasionally. Stir in salt and milk. In a separate small bowl, soften gelatin in ¼ cup water. Add to caramels and stir well. Remove from heat and chill until mixture is thickened. Fold in whipped cream, nuts, and vanilla. Spoon into crust and chill for at least 2 hours in refrigerator. Serves 6 to 8.

The famous Oregon limestone caves were over the "hill" from our little farm on the picturesque Applegate River.

Angel Pie from the Oregon Caves Chateau

"Crust":
4 egg whites
½ tsp cream of tartar
1 cup sugar

Filling (first half):
4 egg yolks
½ cup sugar (scant)
1 tblsp lemon juice
2 tblsps pineapple juice
1 cup fresh grated pineapple

Filling (second half):
1 cup whipping cream
1 tblsp sugar

Preheat oven to 275 degrees.

To make "crust":
In a medium bowl on your mixer, beat egg whites until stiff, gradually adding in the cream of tartar and sugar. Grease and flour a 9 or 10-inch pie pan well and spread egg white mixture on bottom and sides. Bake for 20 minutes. Increase heat to 300 and bake for an additional 40 minutes. "Crust" should be set and very light brown. Cool.

To make Filling (first half):
In the top of your double boiler, combine together the egg yolks, sugar, lemon juice, and pineapple juice. Cook over medium heat until mixture thickens. Stir in pineapple. Cool.

To make Filling (second half):
In a deep bowl on your mixer, whip together the cream and 1 tablespoon sugar. Spoon half into egg white "crust", cover with pineapple filling, then cover all with remaining whipped cream. Serves 6 to 8.

This is a recipe of unknown age, rumored to be from the 1800s and cherished certainly for generations. The place of origin is New Orleans.

Mama Pleasant's Sugar Baby Pie

Pastry for single crust, 9-inch pie (See pages 8-9)
1 egg
¼ tsp baking powder
2 cups sugar
1 tsp vanilla
½ pint (1 cup) heavy cream

Preheat oven to 350 degrees.

Make the standard pie crust adding the egg and baking powder for extra richness. Line pie pan. The original recipe says to combine sugar, vanilla, and cream with a fork in the unbaked pie crust being careful not to tear the pastry. Do this, or mix in a small bowl and pour into crust. The crust will absorb some of the filling. Bake until filling is set, about 30 minutes. Test with a butter knife. Serves 6 to 8.

For devotees of rich creamy chocolate pies, the credit for this delight goes to the Aztec Indians of Mexico. The chocolate as we know it undergoes many processes to take the cacao tree pods and transform it into the flavoring we so love. The Aztecs held chocolate in such high esteem it was often used to pay taxes. The first U.S. manufacturer of chocolate was in the town of Milton Lower Mills, near Dorchester, Massachusetts, in 1765.

Three-Alarm Chocolate Pie

"Crust":

1/3 cup shortening

1 cup all-purpose flour, sifted

1/4 tsp salt

1/2 square semisweet chocolate, grated

2 tblsps ice water

Filling:

1 envelope unflavored gelatin

1/4 cup sugar

1/4 tsp salt

1 tsp instant coffee

1 cup milk

3 egg yolks, beaten

3 squares unsweetened baking chocolate

1/2 tsp vanilla

3 egg whites

1/4 tsp cream of tartar

1/4 cup sugar

2 cups whipping cream

1/2 square semisweet chocolate

Preheat oven to 400 degrees.

In a medium bowl, combine shortening, flour, and salt. Mix in grated semisweet chocolate and sprinkle in 2 tablespoons ice water. Mix only until dough sticks together. Roll out and line a 9-inch pie pan. Bake for 12 minutes and cool.

In a saucepan, mix together gelatin, sugar, salt, and coffee. Blend in milk, egg yolks, and unsweetened chocolate. Cook over low heat, stirring constantly, until chocolate is melted and mixture thickens. Do not let it boil. Pour into a bowl and stir in vanilla. Cool. Filling should be very thick. In a separate bowl, beat egg whites with cream of tartar until foamy. Slowly add in 1/4 cup sugar until whites become stiff peaks. In a separate bowl, whip cream until stiff. Set aside 1 cup of whipped cream for garnish. Beat cooled chocolate mixture until smooth and fold in egg whites and then whipped cream. Pour into the chilled crust and cool an hour or so in refrigerator. Garnish with remaining whipped cream and grate the 1/2 square of semisweet chocolate over top. This pie is very rich and worth the work. Serves 6 to 8.

There are numerous versions of this long-time favorite pie. Although the recipe seems complex, after you've put this together a few times it turns into an easy assembly line. The result is so luscious and delicate you won't mind the little extra work

Louisiana Hotel Black Bottom Pie

Crust:
14 gingersnap cookies, crushed
5 tblsps melted butter

Filling:
1 tblsp plain gelatin
4 tblsps cold water
1¾ cups milk
½ cup sugar
1 tblsp cornstarch
⅛ tsp salt
4 egg yolks

Chocolate Layer:
2 squares (oz.) semi-sweet baking chocolate
1 tsp vanilla

Rum Layer:
4 egg whites
⅛ tsp cream of tartar
½ cup sugar
2 tblsps rum

Topping:
1 cup whipping cream
2 tblsps powdered sugar
1 tblsp grated semi-sweet chocolate

Preheat oven to 300 degrees.

In a medium bowl, mix together the crushed cookies and melted butter. Press crumb mixture into a 9-inch pie pan and bake for 10 minutes. Cool.

In a small dish, dissolve gelatin in cold water. Set aside. In a medium saucepan, scald milk and add in ½ cup sugar. Separately mix cornstarch with salt and beaten egg yolks and add into milk mixture. Cook in a double boiler, stirring constantly, until mixture thickens. Stir in gelatin. Divide this custard in half. Melt chocolate, stir in vanilla, and mix with half the custard. Pour into baked pie shell. Tip pan around so chocolate coats all sides. Cool remaining half of custard. Beat egg whites with cream of tartar, adding in sugar a little at a time, until stiff. Fold into remaining custard. Stir in rum. Spread over chocolate layer. Chill well, overnight if possible. Before serving, whip heavy cream until stiff, adding in powdered sugar slowly, and pile over top of pie. Grate chocolate over this. Serves 6 to 8.

South Carolina Sweet Potato Pie

3 medium-sized sweet potatoes, washed

2 quarts water, approximately

¼ cup (½ stick) butter

2 eggs, separated

½ cup honey

¼ tsp salt

¼ tsp nutmeg

1 tsp baking soda

½ cup milk

½ tsp grated orange rind

1 tsp brandy extract

Pastry for 9-inch pie (See pages 8-9)

3 tblsps sugar

Preheat oven to 450 degrees.

Place potatoes in a 3-quart saucepan with water. Bring to a boil, then reduce to a simmer. Cover pan and cook until potatoes are tender. Drain, skin, and press through a sieve or food processor. Cool a little. In a large bowl, beat together butter, egg yolks, honey, salt, and nutmeg until mixture is creamy. Add in baking soda, milk, orange rind, and extract. Fold in potatoes. Pour mixture into unbaked pie shell and bake 15 minutes. Reduce heat to 300 and continue baking 25 to 30 minutes. Pie should be set. Remove from oven. While pie is baking, beat egg yolks with 3 tablespoons sugar until stiff. Spread evenly over baked pie, making sure meringue seals edges all around. Return to oven for 20 minutes more to lightly brown. Remove and cool. Let cool 2 to 3 hours before cutting. Serves 5 or 6.

Big Sky Country Company Pie

1½ cups canned or cooked pumpkin

1 cup brown sugar, firmly packed

½ tsp ground allspice

1 tsp ground cinnamon

1 tsp ground nutmeg

3 eggs, beaten

1 cup evaporated milk

Pastry for single crust, 9-inch pie (See pages 8-9)

Preheat oven to 425 degrees.

Combine together pumpkin, brown sugar, allspice, cinnamon, and nutmeg. Beat in eggs. Slowly add canned milk. Mix well. Pour into pie crust and bake for 15 minutes. Reduce heat to 350 degrees and continue baking another 35 to 45 minutes. Test by poking butter knife in center. If it comes out clean, it's done. Cool. Serve with a dollop of whipped cream or ice cream. Serves 6 to 8.

Heartland Butterscotch Pie

½ cup butter

1¼ cups brown sugar, firmly packed

1½ cups boiling water

4 tblsps cornstarch

3 tblsps flour

½ tsp salt

1 cup milk

4 egg yolks, beaten

1½ tsp vanilla

Pastry for single crust, 9-inch pie, baked (See pages 8-9)

1 cup heavy cream

½ tsp vanilla

1 tblsp sugar

Using a good heavy saucepan, melt butter over low heat and continue stirring until butter is lightly browned. Stir in brown sugar and boiling water. Bring to a boil and continue boiling for 2 minutes, stirring constantly. In a small dish, combine cornstarch, flour, and salt. Gradually stir in milk until mixture is smooth. Stir into brown sugar mixture, stirring constantly until mixture comes back to a boil. Cook another 5 to 7 minutes until thick. Spoon out about ¼ cup of hot mixture into egg yolks and mix well. Stir this into the brown sugar custard and cook another minute. Remove from heat and stir in vanilla. Cool. Pour into baked pie crust and chill. When ready to serve, whip heavy cream with vanilla and sugar until soft peaks form and offer as topping. Serves 6 to 8.

This recipe was an heirloom at the turn of the century. The general opinion of the Wisconsin family who serve this at family get-togethers is that it tastes like penuche candy.

Green Tomato Pie

Pastry for double crust, 9-inch pie (See pages 8-9)

3 cups green tomatoes, washed, thinly sliced

1½ cups sugar

¼ tsp salt

¼ tsp ground cinnamon

5 tsps grated lemon rind

5 tblsps lemon juice

2 tblsps butter

Preheat oven to 350 degrees.

Line pie pan with bottom crust. Arrange tomatoes around in layers. In a medium bowl, mix together sugar, salt, cinnamon, lemon rind and juice. Sprinkle each layer with the sugar mixture and top off with dots of butter. Seal and crimp on top crust, cut steam vents. Bake for 35 to 40 minutes until crust is light brown and filling is bubbly. Serves 5 to 6.

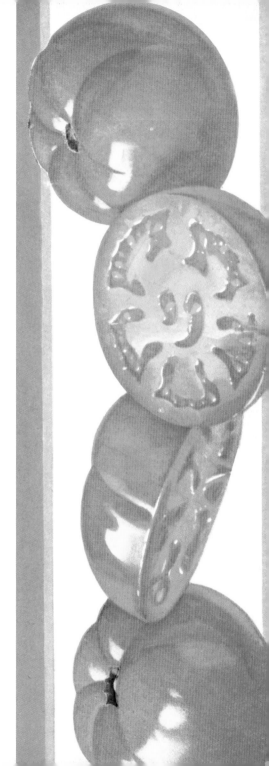

Mid-Winter Homestead Squash Pie

Pumpkin and other squash pies were an obvious winter treat and substitute for fruit. From the time of the first Thanksgiving, the only fruit left after harvest were dried apples, and perhaps plums and cranberries. The winter squash could be stored for months and was a staple of the colonists' diet. The number of varieties is now huge and includes many wonderfully sweet, delicately flavored, and fine textured squash like Delicata, Sugar Baby, Butternut, Buttercup, Turk's Cap, Blue Hubbard and more.

Mid-Winter Homestead Squash Pie

3 eggs

1¼ cups cooked winter squash

1 cup brown sugar, packed

3 tblsps molasses

1 tsp butter

1 tsp ground ginger

1 tsp ground cinnamon

¼ tsp nutmeg

½ tsp salt

1 cup milk

Pastry for single-crust, 9-inch pie (See pages 8-9)

Preheat oven to 325 degrees.

In a medium bowl, beat the eggs. Add in squash, brown sugar, molasses, butter, ginger, cinnamon, nutmeg, salt, and milk. Pour into unbaked pie shell and bake for 325 for 30 to 40 minutes. Pie should be set like a custard. Serves 5 to 6.

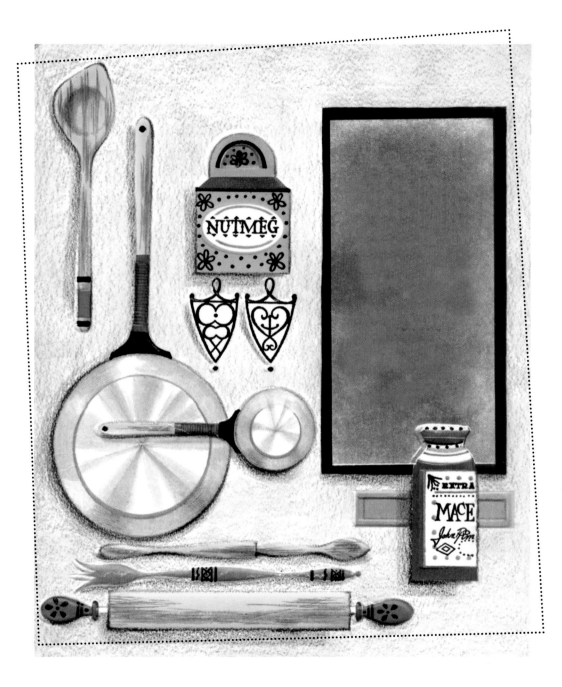

Blue Mountain Traditional Custard Pie

4 cups milk

8 eggs

2 cups sugar

2 tblsps cornstarch

1 tsp vanilla

1/4 tsp salt

Pastry for single-crust, 9-inch pie (See pages 8-9)

Preheat oven to 300 degrees.

In the top of a double-boiler, heat milk almost to a boil (you can do this in a saucepan but there is always the risk of scorching). Remove from heat. Scoop out 1/2 cup of the milk, and let cool a few minutes. In a separate bowl, beat the eggs with this milk and return to milk in double boiler. Blend in well. Add in sugar, cornstarch, vanilla, and salt. Stir to mix completely. Pour milk mixture into unbaked pie shell and bake for 30 to 40 minutes. Custard should be set so that when you poke a butter knife in the center it comes out clean. Serves 4 to 6.

Buttermilk Sky Pie (1880 recipe)

1 1/2 cups brown sugar, packed

1 1/2 cups white sugar

1/2 cup (1 stick) butter, softened

2 tblsps all-purpose flour

6 eggs

1/2 cup buttermilk

1 1/4 tsps vanilla

1/2 tsp salt

Pastry for 2 single-crust, 8-inch pies (See pages 8-9)

Preheat oven to 350 degrees.

In a medium bowl, cream together brown sugar, white sugar, and butter. Beat in the flour, eggs, buttermilk, vanilla, and salt. Pour into the 2 unbaked pie shells and bake for about 30 minutes. Check with a butter knife. Do not over bake as this will make filling watery. Makes 2 pies.

index

Crust

Crumb Crust 9

Gramma Griffin's Favorite Pie Dough 8

Old Faithful Dough 8

Yesteryear Pie Dough.................................8

Main Dish Pies

Alaskan Tundra Partridge Pie 20

Blackbird's Singin' Pie 27

Cape Cod Company Pie.............................17

"Chicken-Pye" 24

Colonial Chicken Pie 25

Creole Pork Pie 30

Garden Delight Veggie Pie 20

Hunter's Reward 21

Kansas Sunday Chicken Pie 24

Miz Lizzie's Chess Pie 37

Mystic Seaport Calm Pie.............................16

New England Leftover Turkey Pie.............31

New England Portside Pie.........................16

Old Arkansas Boiled Egg Pie 28

Old Sturbridge Clam Pie............................16

Oregon Trail's Best Pie...............................32

Oysterville's Pride 18

Simple Cheese Pie 35

Southwest Tamale Pie 33

Steak and Kidney Pie from Fox N'
     Hounds Tavern...18

Wintery Favorite Onion Pie 23

Fruit Pies

Alaskan Candied Rhubarb Pie....................50

Alaskan Wild Berry Pie 70

Amish Sour Cherry Pie...............................56

Applegate River Blackberry Pie.................69

Beacon Hill Apple Pie.................................46

Chattahooche County Pecan Pie 81

Country Bridge Mincemeat Pie.................76

Deep Dish Plum Pie....................................59

Deep South Peanut Butter Pie...................83

Early Autumn Grape Pie.............................53

Family Reunion Walnut Pie 87

Floridian Macaroon Pie 78

Great Aunt Eleanor's Maple-Nut Pie 84

Hannibal, Mississippi Apple Pie 47

Heritage Orchard Traditional Cherry Pie...57

Homesteader's Oatmeal Pie.......................78

Impossibly Perfect Pear Pie........................54

Martha's Cherry Pie....................................55

Meriwether County Glazed Peach Pie 65

Mock Mincemeat Pie 77

Peninsula Surprise Pie 66

Pennsylvania Dutch Raisin Pie 71

Pink Kiss Rhubarb Pie 49

Pope's Ferry Inn Chocolate/Peanut Pie.....88

President Buchanan's Grape Pie 62

Red Brick Café's Banana Cream Pie 63

Rouge Valley Streusel Pear Pie 60

Savannah Anna's Pumpkin Pie 89

Schnitz Pie..40

Schoolmarm's Strawberry Pie......................39

Shaker Hill Pecan Pie 80

Shoo-Fly Pie..73

Sweet Spring Cherry Pie..............................58

Texarkana, Texas Praline Pie.......................84

Turn-of-the-Century Apricot or
    Prune Pie 72

Virginia Real Whiskey Apple Pie.................47

Washington Irving's Mincemeat Pie 75

Custard Pies

Abe Lincoln's Favorite Lemon Pie..............92

Absolutely Perfect Meringue......................91

Angel Pie from the Oregon Caves
Chateau 107

Aunt Mable's Connecticut Lemon Pie 95

Big Sky Country Company Pie..................115

Boone's Kentucky Tavern Lemon Pie........94

Blue Mountain Traditional Custard Pie....124

Buttermilk Sky Pie...................................124

Front Porch Sweet Cheese Pie 102

Grange Apple-Custard Pie 103

Grange Blue-Ribbon Caramel Pie 106

Green Tomato Pie 119

Heartland Butterscotch Pie 116

Land Rush Molasses Pie 98

Louisiana Hotel Black Bottom Pie............113

Mama Pleasant's Sugar Baby Pie 109

Mid-Winter Homestead Squash Pie 120

Pineapple Cream Pie from the
Colonial Inn...101

South Carolina Sweet Potato Pie 114

Three-Alarm Chocolate Pie 111

Webster County Vinegar Pie......................97